Studies

in

Genesis

Studies

in Genesis

John P. Burke

BMH Books
Winona Lake, Indiana 46590

Dedication

To you,
my precious wife, Shirley,
for bringing so much joy to me,
and for your constant example to me

Cover photo by H. Armstrong Roberts

ISBN: 0-88469-048-2

COPYRIGHT 1978
BMH BOOKS
WINONA LAKE, INDIANA

Printed in U.S.A.

Foreword

This study guide on the Book of Genesis is one of a series that covers the books of the Bible, as well as a number of topical studies on Christian truths. The overall plan is to provide study groups, adult Sunday School classes, and formal classes with an adequate guide to challenge students both spiritually and intellectually.

This particular book is intended as a survey of the Book of Genesis. The student will find it helpful to understand the Book of Beginnings. Until a grasp of Genesis can be attained, there is no way of understanding what the rest of the Bible is all about.

In fact, Genesis will help explain your daily newspaper for you! There is evidence of trouble and problems in almost every item you read; or you saw and heard on the evening news telecast. Genesis tells you why mankind is in trouble, how mankind came into beginning and even where mankind is going. It is all in Genesis. The author takes one more step to make the book fit into a context. The last chapter of the book projects you from Genesis through the rest of the Bible in a forward thrust of time right up to eternity.

Rev. John Burke is an experienced Bible teacher and pastor. His practical look at Genesis will be of help to you spiritually. Your understanding will be enlightened and your spirit refreshed as you study this very important book of the Bible.

Charles W. Turner
Executive Editor, BMH Books

Table of Contents

1 Genesis 1:1-25

In the Beginning

INTRODUCTION

STUDY GOAL

EXPOSITION

    I.   **Introduction to the Book**
        A.   The title of the book.
        B.   The human author of the book.
        C.   The structure of the book.

    II.   **God Is the Creator of Light (Gen. 1:1-5)**
        A.   The fact of creation (1:1).
        B.   The date of the creation.
        C.   The manner of creation.
        D.   The first day's creation (1:3-5).

    III.   **God Is the Garnisher of the Earth (Gen. 1:6-13)**
        A.   The formation of the firmament (1:6-8).
        B.   The appearance of land, sea, and plant life.

    IV.   **God Is the Provider of Human Needs (Gen. 1:14-25)**
        A.   The formation of the heavenly bodies (1:14-19).
        B.   The appearance of animal life (1:20-25).

CONCLUSION

INTRODUCTION

The Book of Genesis has often been called, "The Book of Beginnings." This statement is not just a clever saying written by some learned theologian. Instead, the Book of Genesis is the "Book of Beginnings" because it tells us of the beginnings of many different things. For example, in this book is recorded: the beginning of the material universe, the beginning of the earth with all of its various forms of life, the beginning of man, the beginning of human sin, the beginning of the plan of redemption, the beginning of marriage and the home, the beginning of man-made civilization, the beginning of languages, and the beginning of the Hebrew nation. All of these things (and many more) have their beginnings in the Book of Genesis.

Genesis has also been called, "The Seed Plot of the Bible." This statement, too, is not just a clever saying invented by some learned man. Instead, it is called "the Seed Plot of the Bible" because in Genesis practically every important doctrine of Scripture can be found in germ form. For example: the doctrine of the Trinity, the doctrine of man, the doctrine of sin, the doctrine of Satan, the doctrine of election, the doctrine of salvation, the doctrine of justification by faith, the doctrine of separation, and the doctrine of the coming Antichrist are all found in germ form in Genesis. These truths, then, are developed in greater detail throughout the rest of the Bible, but they all have their beginnings in this first book of God's Word.

STUDY GOAL

This chapter is designed to impress the reader with the fact that God is the personal Creator of all that exists.

EXPOSITION

I. Introduction to the Book

Before moving into the text itself, it will be good for us to look at some rather general things about the Book of Genesis. Several things need to be considered.

A. The title of the book. In Old Testament days, the Hebrews gave this book the title, *In the Beginning*. This title, of course, was taken from the opening phrase of the first verse of the book. The Book of Genesis continued to be known by this ancient title until the writing of the Septuagint, a Greek translation of the Old Testament. At the time of the writing of the Septuagint, however, the translators gave the book its present title, *Genesis*, which simply means "origin" or "beginning." From that day to this, the book has continued to be known by this title.

B. The human author of the book. Although the book itself does not reveal who the human author may have been, Bible believers almost unanimously believe that Moses was the human author. The Mosaic authorship of Genesis, of course, has been questioned and rejected by the critics of the Bible. The critics claim that Genesis, as well as the entire Pentateuch, was written by a group of unknown priests or editors about the eighth century B.C. The claim is also made that the Book of Genesis is put together in much the same way as a patchwork quilt—a piece here and a piece there from a rag bag of fragments. While many men believe this view, there isn't a shred of evidence for its support. Instead, the Mosaic authorship of Genesis seems to be clear from such passages as Luke 24:44 and John 5:45-47. This is not to say that Moses may not have used some of the original writings of his day. Moses may have had access to many ancient records and he may have used them. But in all of it, the Holy Spirit carefully guarded and guided Moses even to the choice of every single word.

C. The structure of the book. The book divides into two great sections. The first section includes chapters 1 to 11, and the second section takes in chapters 12 to 50. In the first main section of the book, chapters 1 to 11, there are *four outstanding events:* the Creation, the Fall, the Flood, and the

Babel Crisis. In the second main section of the book, chapters 12 to 50, there are *four outstanding characters:* Abraham, Isaac, Jacob, and Joseph. In our treatment of the Book of Genesis, it is not our intention to cover every chapter and verse. But we will want to concentrate on these outstanding *events* and *characters* as indicated in the outline above.

II. God Is the Creator of Light (Gen. 1:1-5)

These verses are simply filled with teaching truth, and a careful consideration of them will yield rich dividends. Several things ought to be noted.

A. The fact of creation (1:1). This first verse of the Bible is without question one of the most sublime statements that can be found anywhere in the Word of God. This verse is also one of the most important verses in the Bible. It has been well said that what a man does with the entire Bible is determined by what he does with this first sentence. The Bible opens with the simple statement, "In the beginning God created the heaven and the earth." If a man can believe this, he will not have any difficulty believing such things as miracles, prophecies, and evidences of the supernatural. If, however, a man refuses to accept this first statement of Scripture, he will find stumbling blocks in practically every chapter of the Word of God.

The first statement of Scripture is also a simple, concise statement of fact explaining how the universe came into being. Since the very beginning of time, man has been interested in the origin of the universe. Science today has all sorts of ingenious theories as to how matter, as we know it, came into its present form, but it has no explanation as to how the universe came into being in the first place. Even Charles Darwin, the originator of the theory of organic evolution, had to admit: "The beginning of the universe is an unsolvable mystery." Charles Darwin, of course, was not correct in his answer. While science may not have the answer to this question of the origin of the universe, the Bible does have the answer.

The simple teaching of the first verse of the Bible is that the universe is a product of the creative hand of a personal God.

B. The date of the creation. At this point, several questions present themselves. To begin with, we ask, "What is the date of creation? How old is the universe? *When* did God create the heaven and the earth?" In answer to the question, let it be noted at the outset that the Bible nowhere gives us a hint as to the exact date. Someone has well said that the Bible gives us the *Who* and the *what* and the *why* of creation. It tells us a little about the *how* of creation, but it says nothing about the *when*. Though the Bible says nothing about the exact date of creation, for thousands of years man has been trying to find the answer. In the seventeenth century, Bishop James Ussher placed the date of creation at 4004 B.C. This date was determined by adding together the ages of the men listed in the various genealogies of the Old Testament. This date can be found in the margin of many English Bibles today.

The scientist has also attempted to find the answer to this question of the age of the universe. Many astronomers, geologists, chemists and physicists, using many different methods, are saying that the earth is billions of years old. It is rather interesting to notice, however, that even the scientists do not agree among themselves on this matter. In fact, the scientists disagree among themselves to the extent of billions of years! It sounds almost like the scientists are handling the years like the government handles money!

What is to be our answer to this question, as Christians? Is the universe billions of years old, as the scientist claims? Or is the universe of more recent origin? Evangelical Christians have presented several theories to try to reconcile these two widely divergent viewpoints.

1. The first interpretation is the "gap" or "reconstruction" theory which is popular among many evangelicals. This viewpoint is explained in the footnotes of the Scofield Reference Bible. Men who hold to this view say there is a great gap in

time between Genesis 1:1 and 1:2, and the ages of geology fill in this gap. Genesis 1:1 is said to describe an original creation when God created the heaven and earth in a well-formed, perfect condition. Later on, a catastrophe occurred (the catastrophe that is usually suggested for this is the fall of Satan and God's judgment upon him and the angels that fell). (See Isa. 14:12-15; Ezek. 28:11-19.) The creative week of Genesis 1:3, then, is said to be really a period of "recreation" when God "remade" His creation that had been marred by sin.

2. A second interpretation is the "day-age" theory which has gained in popularity in recent years. Men who hold to this view say that the creation of Genesis 1 was the original creation. However, this view teaches that the six days of creation were not 24-hour days, but were actually long periods of time. The various ages of geology are then fitted into this "long week."

3. A third view is the "pictorial day" theory. Those who believe this idea say that the "days" of Genesis 1 have nothing to do with the creation. Instead, they indicate a sequence in revelation. That is, each day is like a lantern slide which God showed to Moses. On the first day, for example, God revealed to Moses the truths of verses 1 to 5, on the second day verses 6 to 8, and so on.

4. Still a fourth view of Genesis 1 might be termed the "recent creation with the appearance of antiquity" theory. According to this view, the entire universe was created within a period of seven literal days (see Exod. 20:11). At the time of the creation, however, God created the universe with the appearance of antiquity. That is, God created the universe with the appearance of great age. When God created Adam, He created him not as a baby, but as a full-grown man. In like manner, the universe had the appearance of age when it left the creative hand of God. According to this theory, the universe is of recent origin and all the fossil remains which are in the earth are the result of great catastrophes since the days of

Adam, and especially the result of the great flood of Noah's day. The flood was a universal affair—and one which had overwhelming geological significance. This position is supported by many strong Biblical arguments and has much to commend it. Anyone interested in doing further research on the subject will find the book *The Genesis Flood,* by Henry M. Morris and John C. Whitcomb, of great help.

C. The manner of creation. A second question that perhaps deserves some discussion has to do with the manner of creation. *How* did God create the heaven and the earth? This question, too, is answered in part in this opening section of Genesis 1. In verse 1, the Bible says that "God *created* the heaven and the earth." This statement not only tells us that God was the originator of the material universe, but it also gives us just a hint as to *how* it was accomplished. The word "created" is the Hebrew word *bara* which means literally "to bring into existence out of nothing." (The same word occurs in verses 1, 21, 26-27.) This apparently means that before God began to create, there was nothing. God had no existing materials to work with. Instead, He simply formed the universe out of nothing. See also Romans 4:17 and Hebrews 11:3.

There are several other references in the New Testament which add light on this subject. In Hebrews 11:3 we are told that "the worlds were framed *by the word of God.*" In Psalm 33:6, the Psalmist says, "*By the word of the Lord* were the heavens made." In Psalm 33:9, the Psalmist adds this further statement, "For he spake, and it was done; he commanded, and it stood fast." These verses, and others like them, would teach us that God simply *spoke* the worlds into being. He apparently did not labor and toil and exhaust Himself. Instead, He merely gave the word, and it was done.

There is yet a third series of references in the New Testament which gives even further light on our question. John 1:3 says, "All things were made by him [Christ]; and without him was not any thing made that was made." The same truth is stated in John 1:10; Colossians 1:16; and Hebrews 1:2. These verses would teach us that the worlds were spoken into existence by the Eternal Son of God, the Lord Jesus Christ. Though every member of the Godhead doubtless had a part in the creation, the Eternal Son seems to be the one member of the Godhead who was given the preeminence.

D. The first day's creation (1:3-5). One other thing is to be noted from this section. In verses 3 to 5 we are told that the first thing God did to prepare the earth for man was to call light into being. He spoke the word, and physical light came into being. These verses would certainly teach us that God is the source of physical light. But we ought to also be reminded that God is the source of spiritual light as well. "For God, who commanded the light to shine out of darkness, hath shined in our hearts, to give the light of the knowledge of the glory of God in the face of Jesus Christ" (II Cor. 4:6). The same power that broke the powers of darkness and brought physical light into being can today break the powers of spiritual darkness and flood our hearts with the glory and light of heaven.

III. God Is the Garnisher of the Earth (Gen. 1:6-13)

In these verses we are told how God prepared the earth for the coming of man. Preparations were made in at least two areas.

A. The formation of the firmament (1:6-8). Our English word "firmament" would seem to suggest something that is "firm" or "solid." This thought of firmness is not involved in the meaning of the word, but it was that misunderstanding that led many during the Middle Ages to the ridiculous idea that the sky was like a great bowl turned upside down over the earth with the stars fastened to the underneath side and with holes in it through which God could pour the rain! The word "firmament," however, has nothing to do with firmness. Instead, the word "firmament" means literally "an expanse" and doubtless refers to the limitless expanse of space above us.

In this connection, it is rather interesting to note in verse 7 that this firmament "divided the waters which were *under* the firmament from the waters which were *above* the firmament." Bible students are not agreed as to what this means, but many believe that God took the waters which enveloped the earth and made two oceans out of them. One ocean He left on the earth, and the other He suspended over the earth above the atmospheric heavens. According to this viewpoint, "the waters which were above the firmament" do not refer to the clouds filled with moisture, but refer to an actual body of water which God suspended over the earth. Later, during the flood, these waters were released and were poured out on the earth. In Genesis 7:11 we are told that in Noah's day, "the fountains of the great deep [were] broken up, and the windows of heaven were opened." The opening of the "windows of heaven" may mean that these waters, suspended over the earth, were released and allowed to flood the earth. If so, then obviously since the days of the flood this great body of heavenly waters has been no more.

B. The appearance of land, sea, and plant life. After dividing the waters on the earth from the waters above the earth on the second day, the whole earth was still probably covered with water. On the third day, God decreed that the waters under the heaven should be gathered into one place. Just how this was done is uncertain, but this may mean that the earth's crust moved, causing the continents to rise above the waters. The waters then drained into the resulting lowlands. After the dry land appeared above the surface of the water, plant life could then begin to grow. So, on this third day God also commanded that plant life appear.

In this section we certainly ought to see the providence of God. The formation of these various things was simply a part of God's plan to prepare the earth for the coming of man. It is good to know that God not only created man, but He also made adequate preparations in every area for his happiness and well-being.

IV. God Is the Provider of Human Needs (Gen. 1:14-25)

These verses describe for us the further provisions which God made for the coming of man who would dwell on the earth. Once again, provisions are made in at least two areas.

A. The formation of the heavenly bodies (1:14-19). Many have attempted to laugh these verses out of the Bible. Men have said, "How could there be light on the first three days when the sun and other heavenly bodies did not appear until the fourth day?" Some have answered this by saying that God illuminated the earth with some kind of light other than sunlight. Another possible answer may be that the sun and other heavenly bodies were included in the creative act of Genesis 1:1. The light of these heavenly bodies, however, may have been obscured by a dense blanket of clouds (see Gen. 1:2). On this fourth day God may have removed this dense blanket of clouds, and the light was permitted to flood the earth.

It is also interesting to note in verse 14 one of the purposes for these "lights." "Let them be for signs, and for seasons, and for days, and years." These words are literally true. The heavenly bodies move on a split second timetable, and the precision of these movements is so perfect that men can use the motions of the heavenly bodies to establish the correct time. These things ought to cause us to fall to our knees in wonder and awe, but the tragedy is that so many refuse to see in the creation the hand of a personal, loving God (see Rom. 1:20-21).

B. The appearance of animal life (1:20-25). These verses clearly teach us that life as we know it has one source, and that one source is God. Foolish men, of course, have invented all sorts of fantastic theories as to how life as we know it has reached its present form, but there has been no answer as to where life came from in the first place.

A Bible teacher was speaking to an evolutionist one day.

He asked him where a chicken's egg came from. "Why, from a hen, of course," replied the young man. "And where does a hen come from?" asked the teacher. "Why, from an egg," responded the young man. The teacher then asked, "Tell me, which came first, the hen or the egg?" "The hen, of course." "Then," said the teacher, "there must have been a hen that existed at one time that didn't come from an egg." The young man was confused. He said, "No, I was wrong, I should have said that the egg was first." "Then," said the teacher, "there must have been an egg that existed at one time that didn't come from a hen." By this time, the young man was thoroughly confused, and in his confusion said, "No—I was right the first time. The hen came first." The teacher, recognizing the young man's confusion, said, "Now, son, tell me. If the hen came first, who made that first hen from which all succeeding eggs and hens have come?" The young man, of course, had no answer because it is impossible to explain any kind of life apart from God. Yet foolish man has invented all sorts of fantastic theories as to how all of life evolved from a single-celled animal. How much better just to take God at His word.

CONCLUSION

The truths of this first chapter of Genesis raise an obvious question: "What is the purpose of all of this? Why did God bring the worlds into existence?" Some would answer by saying that the worlds were created for man's enjoyment. This is true in a limited sense, but as far as the Scriptures are concerned, only one answer is given. The ultimate purpose for the creation is to glorify God. Such verses as Isaiah 43:7; Proverbs 16:4; Revelation 4:11; and Colossians 1:16 clearly teach this. These verses also include the creation of man. Man also was created for one primary purpose, that being to glorify his Creator. Because sin came into the world, however, man can glorify God in only one way today. That is by bowing low at the feet of Christ, confessing Him as Lord, and living for His glory daily. Have you taken your place at His feet and acknowledged Him not only as the Creator of the universe, but also as your own personal Lord? If not, He awaits your decision.

2
Genesis 1:26–2:25

In the Image of God

INTRODUCTION

STUDY GOAL

    I.   **God Created Man (Gen. 1:26-27; 2:7)**
        A.   Man was formed by the special creative act of God (1:26-27; 2:7).
        B.   Man was created in the image of God (1:26-27).
        C.   Man was created male and female (1:27).

    II.   **God Gave Man Responsibility (Gen. 1:26, 28; 2:15)**

   III.   **God Provided for Man**
        A.   Food (1:29).
        B.   Rest (2:1-3).
        C.   A home (2:8-15).

CONCLUSION

INTRODUCTION

Many years ago in the *Sunday School Times,* there appeared a little story about a man who visited a small town on Cape Cod. There he found an old homestead that had not been repaired or cared for in so long that it stood in shambles. As a result, he was able to purchase it for a small sum of money. After purchasing the property, one of the first things the man did to improve it was to hire a man to dig a new well. While they were in the process of digging, however, an aged farmer who had known the place in its original glory asked, "Why don't you open up the old well? There used to be a good well here and it gave plenty of sweet water." The suggestion sounded like a good one, so the workmen began to clean it out. Dirt, stones, rubbish, clay, and sand were all brought to the surface. After a few days of this cleansing process, the old well began to fill up. And to the great joy of the owner, the water proved to be fresh and delicious.

Something of the same might be said of the passage that is to be considered in our lesson for today. "Science" with all sorts of man-made theories, has tried to dump the rubbish of evolution into the waters of this blessed portion of God's Word. The higher critics have sought to destroy it by pouring in the sand of "science, falsely so called." The world, the flesh, and the devil likewise have added their trash to try to clog up its blessed resources. But in spite of these things, the pure water of truth is still here if we will but believe it and receive it.

STUDY GOAL

The goal of this chapter is to present God as the creator and sustainer of human life and to challenge the reader to fit his life into God's plan and purpose. It will not be our purpose to become involved in a long and possibly fruitless attempt to reconcile science and Scriptures. Instead, we will want to concentrate on the moral and spiritual implications of this portion of God's Word.

I. God Created Man (Gen. 1:26-27; 2:7)

Bible scholars have wrestled for centuries with the deep theological truths which are contained in these verses without coming to agreement. No attempt will be made, therefore, to answer all of the questions which might be raised by these verses. Three basic truths, however, do suggest themselves from these verses.

A. Man was formed by the special creative act of God (1:26-27; 2:7). "And God said, Let us make man in our image, after our likeness. . . . *So God created man* in his own image, in the image of God created he him; male and female created he them" (1:26-27). These two verses are a simple statement of fact. In these two verses we are simply told that there was a special consultation between the members of the Trinity. And, after consultation, mankind was brought into being. Further details are then added to this simple statement of fact in Genesis 2:7: "And the Lord God formed man of the dust of the ground, and breathed into his nostrils the breath of life; and man became a living soul." Some have imagined that since there are two different versions of the story of the creation of man, there must have been two creation accounts. In fact, many of the critics of the Bible have said that the first two chapters were written by two entirely different men and that the two accounts are contradictory. This is not true. These two chapters were not written by two entirely different authors. Instead they are the product of one man: Moses. Furthermore, there is no contradiction whatever between Genesis 1 and Genesis 2. Instead, the two chapters are complementary. The creation story of Genesis 2 is but an amplification of the summary statements of Genesis 1.

The two accounts have often been compared to the production of a great painting. The artist first with great sweeping strokes swiftly sketches in the broad outlines. Once this has been done, the artist then returns and begins to fill in the smaller and finer details. This is what Moses has done in these two chapters. In Genesis 1, with great sweeping strokes, Moses has sketched in for us the story of the first six days of creation. Having done this, Moses now returns in Genesis 2 to fill in some of the details. No doubt something of this same thing would be true of these two accounts of the creation of man. In Genesis 1:26 and 27 Moses has given us a brief summary statement of what was involved. In Genesis 2:7 (as well as in Gen. 2:18-22), however, we are given a few of the finer details.

These few verses teach us many things. One fact is especially clear from the text. Man is the product of a special creative act of God. This may not mean that God actually took on human form, and then with physical hands molded a statue of clay, and then, after doing so, blew into the nostrils of the statue to make it alive. Instead, the entire process may have taken place in response to a command from His lips. As in the case of the "worlds which were framed by the Word of God" (Heb. 11:3 lit. trans.), so in like manner God may have simply spoken man into existence. One fact seems to be unmistakably clear: Man was brought into existence by a special creative act of God.

This truth, of course, cuts directly across the "scientific" theories of evolution.

1. The evolutionist claims that billions of years ago lifeless matter, acted upon by natural forces, gave origin to a living organism like a tiny one-celled animal. From this one living organism, all of life as we know it, including man, has since evolved. This, simply stated, is evolution in its basic form.

2. There are others (and some of them are Christians who ought to know better) who hold to a view known as "theistic evolution." Simply stated, theistic evolution is the theory that God originated life and then He supervised the long evolutionary process, intervening at certain points.

Neither of these two theories, however, will stand in the face of the clear evidence of Scripture. Man did not evolve over billions of years from a lower form of life. Nor did God originate and supervise this long evolutionary process. Instead, the clear testimony of the first two chapters of Genesis is that man was formed by a special creative act of God. This same truth is also affirmed in Scripture elsewhere, as in Genesis 5:1-2 and in Matthew 19:4.

B. Man was created in the image of God (1:26-27). Four different times in these two verses it is said that man was made in "the image of God" or in His "likeness." What are we to understand by these terms? What does the Bible mean when it says that we have been created in God's "image" and in His "likeness"? The theologians, of course, have wrestled with this question for centuries. While no attempt will be made to settle all of the debate, the following elements may be involved:

1. Man bears a natural likeness to his creator. By this, it is meant that just as God is a person in the fullest sense of the term, so man is a personality as well. A being who is a person possesses such qualities as the freedom of choice, self-consciousness, and the ability to reason. These qualities are not shared by animals, but they are shared by man and his creator.

2. Man bears a moral likeness to his creator. By this, it is meant that just as God is holy and righteous, so man was created with the capacity for knowing the difference between right and wrong. This quality, once again, is not shared by the animal world. An animal may kill a man, but it cannot be held accountable as a murderer. The moral makeup of man, however, is different. Man does have the capacity for knowing the difference between right and wrong, and therefore can be held accountable for his deeds. This quality is one which man shares with his maker.

3. Man may bear a physical likeness to something in the Godhead which Paul referred to as "the form of God" (Phil. 2:5). The word "form" means "shape" or "external appearance." The physical form of man, without question, is the

most perfect and the most beautiful of all of God's creation. And it would seem that man's physical body must have had as its pattern something in the mind of God. How can this be, when God is pure spirit and has no body? Some have answered by saying that the pattern may have been the body of the incarnate Son of God who came many years later. It would appear that at least this much is involved in the "image of God."

It is likewise clear from Scripture that even since the fall, men possess this image (see Gen. 9:6; James 3:9). It is true that this image has been spoiled and marred by sin, but it is still there. In spite of his sin, man still exists as a person. In spite of his sin, man is still a morally responsible creature. And in spite of his sin, man still bears some resemblance to that pattern after which he was originally fashioned. Though the image has been marred and spoiled by sin, it is still there.

After we have said this much, there is little more that we can say. If all this seems to be too mysterious and too inadequate, then the writer is in perfect agreement! There is much that we do not know. Perhaps for this very reason, the Psalmist exclaimed, "I will praise thee, for *I am fearfully and wonderfully made*; marvellous are thy works; and that my soul knoweth right well" (Ps. 139:14).

C. Man was created male and female (1:27). "So God created man in his own image, in the image of God created he him; *male and female created he them.*" Just what all God may have had in mind in creating mankind as male and female may never fully be known, because of man's fall into sin. Two purposes, however, appear to be rather obvious. To begin with, it ought to be rather obvious that this was God's way of providing for the continuation of the race from generation to generation. Certainly, it was God's intention that families be established and that children be born into the world and that love should reign in the home. In this connection, it is rather interesting to note that in the New Testament the love of husband to wife and vice versa is compared to that relationship which exists between Christ and His church (see Eph. 5:22-23). In the second place, the creation of mankind as male and female must have also been God's way of providing companionship for man. God did not make man to live alone. Instead, man is a social being, as well as a spiritual being—and this was God's way of providing for this particular need.

II. God Gave Man Responsibility (Gen. 1:26, 28; 2:15)

It is rather interesting and significant to note that even before the fall of man in the Garden of Eden God gave Adam a job to do which must have kept him busy. In Genesis 1:26, where we are told that God determined to make man, almost in the next breath the Bible says that he was to be given dominion "over the fish of the sea, and over the fowl of the air, and over the cattle, and over all the earth." In Genesis 1:28 this same thought of dominion is repeated. And finally, in Genesis 2:15 one of man's responsibilities is spelled out. He was to "dress" and "keep" the Garden of Eden. Just what this dressing and tilling consisted of, we do not know. But it was something that kept him busy. In addition, in Genesis 2:19 and 20 he was given the responsibility of naming the various animals and birds. God apparently did not want Adam to be idle. Instead, He wanted him to be kept busy. God, then, gave man work to do even before sin came, and Adam must have thoroughly enjoyed it. When sin came into the world, however, "work" then became "labor." There is a vast difference between "work" and "labor," and the difference is largely a matter of attitude. Work is a wholesome activity which is a beneficial and enjoyable thing. Labor, on the other hand, is a burdensome thing which is not enjoyed. The difference between the two is largely a matter of attitude. If you enjoy your "labor" it ceases to be "labor" and becomes "work." On the other hand if your "work" becomes burdensome to you, it ceases to be "work" and becomes "labor."

Work is still a blessing today. Sometimes men feel as though they would like to get away from work forever and do nothing for the rest of their lives. Experience, however, proves that people like this are not very happy. God made man to work, and under normal conditions there is nothing quite as satisfying as doing the work which God has given us to do. Thomas Carlyle, a famous author, once wrote, "Blessed is he who has found his work; let him seek no other blessedness." Work is also spiritually healthy. As the saying goes, "An idle mind is still the devil's workshop." And experience has proved that when men are idle, immorality and sin usually flourish. If this be true, may we enjoy what we are doing, thank God that we can work, and then do the best job that we can possibly do at the place where He has put us.

III. God Provided for Man

Scattered throughout the remaining parts of our text are indications by the Holy Spirit that certain provisions were made for man. God not only created man and gave him responsibility, but He also generously provided for his needs. Several provisions are to be noted.

A. Food (1:29). "And God said, Behold, I have given you every herb bearing seed, which is upon the face of the earth, and every tree, in the which is the fruit of a tree yielding seed; to you it shall be for meat." It would seem from this verse that man's original diet was a vegetarian diet. In this we ought to see something of the goodness of God. Since man's diet was to be "every herb bearing seed," man would never be able to exhaust the supply, because vegetation reproduces itself. Furthermore, the text says that man's food would be "upon the face of all the earth" which would indicate that man would find food wherever he went. It would always be there. This ought to remind us that in the final analysis it is the Lord who still supplies our physical needs from day to day.

B. Rest (2:1-3). "And God blessed the seventh day, and sanctified it: because that in it he had rested from all his work which God created and made" (2:3). We are not to understand from this section that God needed to rest because He had exhausted Himself during the first six days of creation. God did not rest in this sense. Instead, God rested only in the sense that He ceased or stopped His creative activity. After the sixth day, the work of creation was complete, and so God ceased from His work.

According to the third verse, however, God not only ceased from His labors, but He "blessed the seventh day and sanctified it [set it apart]." For whom was it set apart? Certainly it was not set apart for God's benefit so much as for man's (see Mark 2:27). In this instance, again we ought to see something of the goodness of God in providing for man's need. While men may disagree on which day of the week ought to be observed, as well as the meaning and significance of that day, the principle of one day out of seven for rest is a good one and a healthful one. The physical needs of man simply demand the observance of a weekly day of rest; and when men have tried to work seven days a week without rest, they have discovered that their effectiveness has been greatly limited.

C. A home (2:8-15). "And the Lord God planted a garden eastward in Eden; and there he put the man whom he had formed" (2:8). All sorts of attempts have been made to try to locate the Garden of Eden, and all without success. Perhaps the reason for this is that the flood of Noah's day so completely altered the surface of the earth that the exact spot may never be located—and perhaps this is for the best. It seems that man has been an untiring shrine-builder over the years. And had God allowed Eden to be discovered, man would have ended up worshiping the creation rather than the Creator (see Rom. 1:25).

Once again in this passage we ought to see the goodness of God in providing for man. God not only created man and provided for his happiness and well-being in other areas, but He also provided a beautiful and perfect environment in which to live. The name "Eden" means "delight" or "pleasure." The word "garden" is rendered in the Greek by the word "paradise." These two words give us just a little bit of a hint as to what sort of place this was. What a place of beauty and rest and joy it must have been!

"And the Lord God said, It is not good that the man should be alone; I will make him an help meet for him" (2:18). After providing food, rest, and a home for Adam, one thing was lacking—a companion. And in these verses God provided for this need. Joseph Parker, in his commentary, has well said, "For a man to be alone means suicide; for two men to be together means homicide; woman alone can keep society moving and helpful." Truer words have never been spoken. Emotionally, physically, and socially neither a man nor a woman can face life as satisfactorily alone as when in the company of a mate. God realized this and so provided for this need as well.

It is interesting to note *how* God provided a companion for Adam. To begin with, in verses 21 and 22, we are told that "God caused a deep sleep to fall upon Adam, and he slept [here was the first case of anaesthesia in medical history!]: and he took one of his ribs, and closed up the flesh instead thereof; and the rib, which the Lord God had taken from the man, made he a woman, and brought her unto the man." Eve's creation, as Adam's, may have taken place in a moment of time at the command of God. The point of the verse, however, is that the woman was made from a part of the man thus uniting the human race and making Adam the ancestor of the entire human family, including Eve.

D. L. Moody, a famous preacher of another generation, pointed out that it is rather significant that Eve was taken from Adam's side rather than from another part of his body. Had she been taken from Adam's head, this would have indicated that he was superior to her and she was to be browbeaten by him. Had she been taken from his feet, this would have indicated that she was to be trampled under foot by him. Instead, she was taken from under his arm, indicating that she was to be protected by him; and from near his heart, indicating that she was to be loved by him.

After God fashioned Eve, He brought her to Adam. And what a joy and delight she must have been to him!

This section certainly abounds with truth concerning God's gracious provision for man. God not only formed man, brought him into being, but He graciously provided for his every need.

CONCLUSION

At the conclusion of this section, we ask ourselves, "What is the purpose of all this? Why did God bother to bring man into existence in the first place, and why did He provide for his needs? What was God's goal and objective?" These questions are answered in the first chapter of Ephesians.

"According as he hath chosen us in him before the foundation of the world, *that we should be holy and without blame before him in love*" (Eph. 1:4). "That we should be *to the praise of his glory,* who first trusted in Christ" (Eph. 1:12).

Why was man created in the image of God? What was God's goal and objective? God's purpose for bringing man into being was that he might reflect God's glory. With the coming of sin into the world, however, man can glorify God in only one way, and this is by bowing low at the feet of Christ, confessing Him as Lord, and by living for Him daily. Are you fulfilling this purpose for which you were created? If not, why not take your place at His feet today and begin living daily for His glory?

3 Genesis 3:1-24

~~~~~~

The World's Greatest Tragedy

INTRODUCTION

STUDY GOAL

CONCLUSION

INTRODUCTION

The third chapter of the Book of Genesis is one of the most important chapters of the Word of God. What has often been said of the Book of Genesis as a whole is true of this chapter in particular; it is "the seed plot of the Bible." This is because in this chapter can be found many of the foundation stones upon which our faith rests. In this chapter, for example, we have the explanation of how mankind has reached its present fallen and ruined condition. In this chapter, we learn about the subtle devices of our enemy, the devil. It is here that we learn about the spiritual effects of sin. It is here that we learn about man's universal tendency to try to cover his sin by a work of his own hands. It is here that we learn about God's attitude toward guilty sinners and about His gracious provision which He has made for our need. And it is here in this chapter that a marvelous stream of prophecy begins that runs all the way through the Scriptures. These and a host of other important truths have their beginnings in this chapter. All of this just means that the chapter is one of extreme importance.

STUDY GOAL

The aim of our study is to review this familiar chapter in order to learn from it the origin of sin in the human family, the subtlety of temptation, and the tragic consequences of disobedience to God's Word.

I. Satan's Temptation (Gen. 3:1-5)

This section abounds with teaching truth. Two items in particular, however, are to be noted.

A. The identity of the tempter (3:1). "Now the serpent was more subtil than any beast of the field which the Lord God had made."

If this chapter were the only chapter in the Bible, we might be led to suppose that the tempter mentioned here was a snake, or a member of the animal kingdom, rather than a great evil spirit being called the devil, or Satan. Actually, the word "serpent" ought to be read as a proper name, for the words refers to our archenemy, the devil. The identity of this serpent is given elsewhere in such passages as John 8:44; II Corinthians 11:3; I John 3:8; Revelation 12:9 and 20:2.

Just where this creature came from is not spelled out in the text. Instead, he is just suddenly and unexpectedly introduced here without any explanation as to his origin. Men, of course, have speculated on this subject. Many conservative Bible students, for example, believe that Isaiah 14:12-15 and Ezekiel 28:11-19 describe his origin. While men may disagree on the interpretation of these two passages, it does appear to be clear that Satan as we know him today is a created being rather than an eternal being. This seems to be clear from the first two chapters of the Book of Job, where he is referred to several times as among "the sons of God." If this be true, then the fact that Satan is a created being would imply that somewhere along the line he fell into deep sin as a result of a rebellious free choice, for God canot be made the author of sin. Finally, though the Bible has little to say about Satan's origin, it does spell out for us his ultimate and final destiny. Jesus said in Matthew 25:41 that hell was being prepared for "the devil and his angels." Beyond these few facts, perhaps we dare not speculate.

Just what this creature who spoke to Eve may have looked like is not given in detail. It does appear to be clear, however, that Satan spoke to Eve through an animal that we know today as the serpent. But how could a serpent talk? In answer to the question, it may be helpful to remember that years later God gave Balaam's ass the temporary gift of speech (Num. 22:28). In this chapter Satan in like manner gave the serpent the power to speak. This is a power that apparently Satan possesses, for II Thessalonians 2:9 speaks of his "lying wonders," and Revelation 13:15 speaks of a day yet future when the Antichrist, energized by Satan, will have the power to make an image speak and live. So, on this occasion Satan spoke through an animal to deceive our first parents.

B. The subtlety of the temptation (3:1-5). As one reads these verses, one cannot help but be impressed with the extreme subtlety or cleverness of the tempter. In examining the text carefully, it appears that the temptation came in three distinct steps:

1. To begin with, in the first three verses Satan tempted Eve to *doubt* God's Word. In verse 1, for example, he said to her, "Yea, hath God said?" Notice carefully that Satan did not begin with a flat denial. Instead, he disarmed Eve by sowing the seed of doubt in her heart—doubt concerning God's goodness and His fairness. By this question, "Yea, hath God said?" Satan probably was not attempting to create doubt in Eve's mind as to the *fact* of what God had said, but upon the *fairness* of it. In essence he was saying, "God isn't being fair in placing this demand on you. He doesn't have your best interests at heart." Satan, of course, still uses this same approach today. He keeps many from the gospel message by convincing men that God's demands are too harsh or by convincing them that the Christian faith will interfere with some pleasure of life which they especially enjoy. In this connection now, it is rather interesting to note Eve's reply, "And the woman said . . . We may eat of the fruit of the trees of the garden: But of the fruit of the tree which is in the midst of the garden, God hath said, Ye shall not eat of it, neither shall ye touch it, lest ye die" (3:2-3). Note that Eve made three important changes in God's statement which originally had been given in Genesis 2:16 and 17. First, she omitted the words "every" and "freely" which indicates that she agreed with the devil's suggestion that God was not good. Second, she added the phrase "neither shall ye touch it" which was an exaggeration of God's demands. And third, she toned down the penalty from "in the day thou eatest thereof thou shalt *surely* die" to "lest ye die." Certainly these changes are an indication that Eve was beginning to yield to the devil's temptation to doubt.

2. A second step which Satan took in his temptation was to *deny* God's Word. In verse 4, Satan said flatly, "Ye shall not surely die." Satan now moves from doubt to a flat denial. This, of course, is often Satan's procedure. After he has caused a person to question God's Word, his next step is to get that person to deny its truth. He is still telling sinners today that they will not surely die. A high official in a large Protestant denomination was recently quoted as saying, "As for any eternal punishment, I am sure that God is at least as good and merciful as a man. I certainly would not banish any man to a place of eternal punishment because of his faults. I am sure that God is not less fair!" This was exactly Satan's approach to Eve. After creating doubt in her mind, he now flatly denied a clear statement made by the Lord.

3. As a final step in his approach, Satan now *distorted* God's Word. In verse 5, he said, "God doth know that in the day ye eat thereof, then your eyes shall be opened, and ye shall be as gods, knowing good and evil." It is rather interesting to observe that what Satan said here was true—or at least half true. It was true that Adam and Eve did not "die" in the sense that they dropped dead upon yielding. But, of course, they did die spiritually, a fact that Satan did not bother to mention. It was true that the eyes of Adam and Eve were "opened" when they yielded. But, of course, what they saw when their eyes were opened filled them with shame and regret rather than satisfaction, a fact that Satan did not mention either. And it was true that Adam and Eve did become as "gods" when they yielded, in the sense that from this point on they became morally fixed creatures. But, unfortunately, they became fixed in sin rather than in righteousness, a fact that Satan cleverly left unsaid as well. In every case, Satan perverted and distorted God's Word with only half-truths. This, of course, is still his method today. A half-truth is oftentimes more dangerous than an outright lie, and the devil is a master at this kind of deception.

This section, then, certainly ought to warn us that today

Satan is a clever, subtle creature who has the ability to plan and connive and deceive far beyond our ability to even think or imagine. And if so, then how important it is that we be alert to his devices. See II Corinthians 11:14; I Peter 5:8 and 9.

II. Man's Yielding (Gen. 3:6)

This verse is one of the most tragic verses that can be found anywhere in Scripture. It is not our intent to present an exhaustive treatment of it here. However, at least two important items should be noted.

A. The avenues of temptation (3:6). "The woman saw that the tree was good for food, and that it was pleasant to the eyes, and a tree to be desired to make one wise." These words would seem to indicate that there are three basic avenues through which men are tempted, once the "softening up" process which we have just considered has been completed. First, Satan approached Eve through the physical or bodily appetite. This thought is suggested by the words, "The woman saw that the tree was good for food." Second, Satan appealed to Eve's emotions or to the aesthetic side of her personality. This thought is suggested by the words, "It was pleasant to the eyes." Finally, Satan appealed to Eve's intellect, suggested by the words: "A tree to be desired to make one wise."

It is interesting and significant to recall that in at least two other passages in the Word of God, the Holy Spirit indicates that temptation always falls into these same three categories. In Matthew 4, for example, where we have the account of the temptation of Christ, we discover that our Lord was tempted along the same general lines—the physical, the emotional, and the intellectual. Also, in I John 2:16, the Apostle John has set forth an exhaustive statement of the avenues of temptation with the words: "The lust of the flesh, the lust of the eyes, and the pride of life." It would seem then from these three passages that the temptations of Satan will always approach us from these three avenues. If so, may this truth better enable us to recognize and resist the attacks of the enemy when they come.

B. The act of yielding (3:6). "She took of the fruit thereof, and did eat, and gave also unto her husband with her; and he did eat." Many different interpretations have been given to these words. For example, the prevalent view of this passage among liberal theologians is that the fall of man is just a "myth" and that what we have here is simply a symbolical way of setting forth what happens to every human being. That is, the liberal theologian would say that just as Adam and Eve disobeyed in taking of the forbidden fruit, so men today disobey on occasion. While there is an element of truth here, the view is wrong because it completely overlooks and denies the doctrine of original sin so clearly taught in the Word. See Romans 5:12.

A common interpretation of this verse during the Dark Ages was that the "eating of the fruit" was really the first sexual act ever committed by man. Such an interpretation is horrid beyond description and ought to be strongly denounced. Genesis 1:28 makes it clear that prior to the fall, God Himself gave the command, "Be fruitful and multiply." Furthermore, Hebrews 13:4 should put to silence the advocates of this view once and for all.

These and other interpretations have been given to the actual act involved in the fall. Just exactly what happened we may never know in this world. However, it seems best to this author to interpret the passage just as literally as possible. That is, it seems best to understand these words just as they appear here. There were two literal trees in a literal garden. Our first parents disobeyed God and ate the forbidden fruit of the "tree of the knowledge of good and evil." And as a result, the entire human family was plunged into sin.

Sometimes an objection is raised at this point. Men will ask, "But, how could such a far-reaching penalty be attached to such a harmless, innocent act as this?" The answer is that

Adam's sin involved more than just an outward act. It also involved an inward choice of the will. By taking of the forbidden fruit, Adam voluntarily chose to act independently of God, which is the very essence of sin. The outward act was bad enough, but it was the inward choice of Adam and Eve that made what they did so sinful.

III. Sin's Results (Gen. 3:7-24)

These few verses list a few of the major results of the sin of our first parents, along with their modern-day applications.

A. For the entire human race (3:7-13, 22-24). It is interesting to observe that there were at least three results which took place in Adam's own life almost immediately following his sin.

1. First, because of his sin, Adam became a *guilty* sinner. This sense of guilt is clearly seen in the crude attempts which Adam and Eve made to try to cover their own nakedness (vv. 7-8).

2. Second, because of his sin Adam's heart became *wicked and corrupt.* This is clearly seen in the evasive answers which Adam and Eve gave to God's questions (vv. 9-13).

3. And finally, because of his sin, Adam became *spiritually dead* and so was alienated from God. This thought is seen in man's expulsion from the Garden of Eden (vv. 22-24). So, three tragic results took place in Adam's own life because of his sin: he became a guilty sinner, his heart became wicked and corrupt, and he became spiritually dead and had to be alienated from God.

Needless to say, these same three results have been carried down to every member of the human race. First, because of Adam's sin, we, too, are guilty sinners—for we sinned in him. See Romans 5:12—"Wherefore as by one man sin entered into the world . . . ." and Romans 5:19—"For as by one man's disobedience many were made sinners. . . ." Bible students have debated for centuries over these verses to try to settle the matter of whether Adam was the natural head of the race or the federal head of the race. One's theory of the matter isn't too important. But it is important that men be made to realize that when Adam sinned, we sinned, too, for we were in him. Second, because of Adam's sin, we, too, are wicked and corrupt in heart. In Psalm 51:5 David said, "In sin did my mother conceive me." This does not mean, as some have supposed, that there is something sinful about conception. But it means that the heart of man is wicked and corrupt from the day of his birth. (See also Ps. 58:3; Jer. 17:9; Mark 7:21-23.) The wicked things we do from day to day stem from a wicked heart that can be traced all the way back to Adam's sin. Finally, because of Adam's sin we are spiritually dead and are dwelling under the wrath of a holy God. Ephesians 2:1 says, "And you hath he quickened, *who were dead* in trespasses and sins."

The sin of Adam not only involved himself and his wife, but his disobedience had a devastating effect upon the entire human family as well.

B. For the serpent and Satan (3:14-15). These verses record God's judgment upon the serpent and upon Satan who used this animal as an instrument to carry out his temptation. In verse 14, the serpent is cursed immediately with the words, "Upon thy belly shalt thou go, and dust shalt thou eat all the days of thy life." This statement does not *necessarily* imply that at one time the serpent did not crawl on its belly any more than verse 19 implies that at one time man did not work. Instead, this means that henceforth and forever the serpent crawling in the dust would be a sign of its part in man's sin. It is rather interesting to note in passing that this curse will never be lifted, not even during the millennial age. See Isaiah 65:25. Instead, even during this golden age, the serpent will crawl upon its belly and eat the dust of the earth as an ever-present reminder of the awfulness of sin.

The curse upon Satan, who stood behind the serpent, is given in verse 15. "And I will put enmity between thee and the woman, and between thy seed and her seed, *it,* [the seed of the woman] *shall bruise thy head,* and thou shalt bruise his heel." These words, we believe, have their fulfillment in the coming of the Lord Jesus Christ and His death on the cross. The picture is that of a man killing a snake. Upon seeing a snake, a man will raise his foot and bring his heel down upon its head and utterly crush it. Sometimes, however, at the last moment, the snake will bury its fangs into the man's foot—thus producing a sting or bruise. This is what happened at the cross. At the cross, Satan was given a death blow. See Hebrews 2:14-15. However, in the process, Christ suffered the sting of death. Christ's death, however, did not mean defeat, for through it eternal salvation has been made available to all men.

C. For the woman (3:16). God's curse upon the woman for her part in sin involved at least two things. First, she was to experience pain in childbirth: "I will greatly multiply thy sorrow and thy conception; in sorrow thou shalt bring forth children." If this be true, then every childbirth, with its accompanying difficulty and anguish, is a witness to the fall of man and a constant reminder that all is not well between man and God. Second, because of her part in sin the woman was cursed with a place of subordination and subjection to her husband: "Thy desire shall be to thy husband, and he shall rule over thee." The simplest meaning of these words is that henceforth and forever the woman would be forced to submit her desires and wishes to the will of her husband. Thus, the two things that God intended originally to be sources of great joy and rich blessing—the privilege of childbearing and the companionship of a husband—would now become sources of pain and suffering to the woman because of her part in sin. The evidence of this curse, of course, can be seen clearly today. It is only in areas where the gospel message has been preached that the position of women has been elevated to that which God intended that it be.

D. For the man (3:17-19). These verses do not imply that up to this point man did not work. The facts of the matter are that he did work. See Genesis 2:15, 19 and 20. Up to this point, however, man's work was a source of enjoyment and pleasure to him, for he was kept busy carrying out his God-given tasks. God's curse is that of hard labor. No longer would work be the source of pleasure that it had been. Instead, it now would become a wearisome struggle for survival. Few of us in our land of plenty have any concept of how literally true verses 17 through 19 are in most parts of the world. Such things as extreme poverty, discouraging hard work, and frequent famines are the rule rather than the exception for most of the world's population—a grim reminder of man's fall into sin.

CONCLUSION

This chapter, indeed, could be called "The World's Greatest Tragedy," for every sin, sorrow, heartache, and need that the world has ever known has stemmed from it. Yet how thrilling to realize the truth of Romans 5:20—"But where sin abounded, grace did much more abound." This statement simply means that though man has sinned—and sinned grievously—God's love is strong enough and His power is great enough to overcome the effects of Adam's sin. This is possible through the death of Christ who died as our substitute for sin that we might live. See II Corinthians 5:21. Thank God for the fact of His love! Thank God for the fact of Christ's provision! And thank God for the availability of God's plan of redemption to whosoever will!

4 Genesis 6:1–7:24

Noah and the Flood

INTRODUCTION

STUDY GOAL

I. **The Causes of the Flood (Gen. 6:1-12)**
   A. Unbridled lust (6:1-4).
   B. Wicked thoughts (6:5).
   C. Violent acts (6:11-12).

II. **Preparations for the Flood (Gen. 6:13–7:9)**
   A. The building of the ark (6:13-18).
   B. The gathering of the animals (6:19-22; 7:2-6).
   C. The entering of the ark (7:1, 7-9).

III. **The Judgment of the Flood (Gen. 7:10-24)**

CONCLUSION

INTRODUCTION

In our treatment of the Book of Genesis, no attempt is being made to consider every chapter and verse. Rather, 13 Scripture passages which seem to be significant so far as God's redemptive purpose is concerned, have been selected for study. This will mean, of course, that the "in between" portions, while important in themselves, will not be treated in detail. Instead, emphasis will be placed on the 13 selected "heart passages" which have to do with God's redemptive program.

The section before us is another one of the important "heart passages" of the Book of Genesis. The story of Noah and the flood is an awesome account, and without question it is one of the most important events of human history. If the flood of Noah's day covered the entire globe, as we believe it did, then this event is of tremendous scientific significance and its importance simply cannot be overstated. But not only is the story of Noah and the flood important from a historical and scientific standpoint, we believe that this event is important from a moral standpoint as well. This event ought to stand as an eternal warning to men, that sin will be punished and that righteousness will not go unrewarded. Such an application of this event, of course, has been made in the Scriptures (see II Peter 3:1-7). Further, the flood of Noah's day has also been used in the Word of God to point us to the soon return of our Lord (see Matt. 23:37-39). For these reasons, we ought to have more than just a casual interest in the Genesis account of the flood.

STUDY GOAL

The aim of this study will be to warn men of the certainty of God's judgment if they fail to repent and to encourage them to avail themselves of God's provision of salvation.

I. The Causes of the Flood (Gen. 6:1-12)

This section absolutely abounds with teaching truth. In

fact, multiplied volumes have been written on these verses over the years. No attempt will be made here to deal with all of the problems of the text. Rather, a few of the basic causes of the flood are listed along with the spiritual lessons of the passage.

A. Unbridled lust (6:1-4). "The sons of God saw the daughters of men that they were fair; and they took wives of all that they chose" (6:2). Who were the "sons of God" and the "daughters of men" who are mentioned in these verses? This is a question that is frequently asked. And it is a question which conservative students of the Bible have debated for generations and yet have failed to answer in agreement. It is not our purpose to try to solve this weighty problem. However, the various views on this question might be summarized as follows.

Three different views of this passage have been held from earliest times.

1. First, there have been some who have regarded the "sons of God" mentioned in the text as princes or men of the nobility class and the "daughters of men" as the daughters of just ordinary folk. This view, while held by some of the early church fathers, is no longer held by any known Bible scholar today.

2. A more popular view of this passage is that the "sons of God" were the righteous descendants of Seth (see Gen. 4:25-32), and the "daughters of men" were the ungodly descendants of Cain (see Gen. 4:17-24). Bible students who hold this view say that in Genesis 4 the Cainite line is presented, in Genesis 5 the Sethite line is presented, and finally in Genesis 6 the two lines are joined together in an unholy marriage. And as a result of this union a race of monstrosities was produced. This view is defended in the Scofield Reference Bible and is held by many of the more recent evangelical commentaries.

3. Still a third view of this passage is the view which says that the "sons of God" were fallen angelic beings or perhaps

demons who entered and possessed the bodies of wicked men. The "daughters of men" then were exactly that—ordinary marriageable females. And as a result of this unholy sexual union, the race of monstrosities mentioned in verse 4 was produced.

Of the three views, the last one impresses this writer most for the following reasons: (a) The term "sons of God" is used uniformly in the Old Testament to refer to angelic beings. The term "sons of God" occurs but four times in the Old Testament and in each case the term is used of angelic beings. See Job 1:6; 2:1; 38:7; Daniel 3:25. Consistency would seem to demand that the "sons of God" of Genesis 6 were also angelic beings of some sort. (b) In II Peter 2:4, the Apostle Peter speaks of the "angels that sinned," and because of it he says that God "cast them down to hell [Tartarus]." This statement of Peter's apparently does not refer to the original fall of Satan and his angels back in the beginning, for Peter says that because of this sin God "delivered them [the angels that sinned] into chains of darkness, to be reserved unto judgment." The implication of this statement is that sometime after their original fall into sin, these angels entered into a second and deeper apostasy so wicked and vile that God had to cast them into Tartarus (a special compartment of hell) where they are confined today in chains of darkness awaiting the day of judgment. Peter's statement would seem to fit with Genesis 6. If demons or angelic beings were involved in the sin of Genesis 6, this would easily explain why God would have to judge these angels in this way. Their wickedness would be so great that God would not dare allow them to roam free lest they corrupt the entire human family. It is also rather interesting to note that in the same context, the flood is mentioned. This would seem to imply that the sin of these angels could have taken place in or around the time of the flood (see II Peter 2:5). (c) In Jude, verses 6 and 7, Jude speaks of "angels which kept not their first estate, but left their own habitation." In verse 7 the sin of these angels is described in these words: "Even as Sodom and Gomorrha, and the cities about them in like manner, giving themselves over to fornication, and going after strange flesh . . . ." These words would indicate that the sin of these angels was closely akin to the unnatural vices of Sodom and Gomorrha—fornication of an abnormal kind. This, of course, was exactly the kind of sin which was involved in the horrible story of Genesis 6.

For these reasons, it seems best to this writer to accept the view that the story of Genesis 6 involves an unholy alliance between demon-possessed men or fallen angelic beings and the godless women of that day. Regardless of which view is accepted, however, it does seem to be clear that there was a tragic breakdown in Noah's day on moral and spiritual matters. These were days when all moral restraints were thrown off, a day when lust and immorality prevailed. And as a result, God had to judge and cleanse the earth with a flood. This thought certainly ought to be a warning to us today. We, too, live in a day of unbridled lust and moral looseness. And because of it we, too, may expect that God's judgment will come. When man begins to cast off God's restraints, judgment cannot be too far away.

B. Wicked thoughts (6:5). "God saw that . . . every imagination of the thoughts of his [man's] heart was only evil continually." These words are a tragic commentary on the almost staggering wickedness of Noah's day. Notice, for example, these thoughts from the text.

1. The verse says that *every imagination without exception* was evil.

2. The verse says that every imagination was *only evil,* or nothing but evil. That is, the thoughts of men's hearts were not a mixture made up of some good thoughts and some bad thoughts. Instead, every thought was only evil.

3. The verse says also that every thought was evil *continually.* That is, there were no intermissions in between periods of wicked thinking. Instead, every moment of every

day was filled with ungodly thoughts and wicked imaginations withot any let-up whatsoever. What corruption and rottenness must have been present in Noah's day! Little wonder that the judgment of the flood became necessary.

While this verse is a historical commentary on the wickedness of Noah's day, we believe that it is also an excellent text on the subject of the total depravity of man. This verse describes our own state apart from Christ as well as the condition of every other unconverted sinner in the world today. This is a truth that we need to preach; and unless we preach it, we are not proclaiming a full Gospel. Other passages which teach the same truth are Genesis 8:21, Psalm 51:5, and Jeremiah 17:9.

C. Violent acts (6:11-12). "The earth also was corrupt before God, and the earth was filled with violence" (6:12). The word "violence" that is used here means "highhanded dealings" or "a violation of the rights of others." This may refer to organized crime and lawlessness such as we have today. Or it may refer to individual acts of lawless behavior such as murder, lust, greed, robbery, and utter godlessness. Conduct of this kind, of course, would be the natural outcome of verse 5. Because man's heart and mind were corrupt, a corrupt life and behavior could not help but follow.

This was the day of Noah, and these were some of the reasons for the coming of the floods of judgment upon the earth. As one reads this scriptural account, one cannot help but see a parallel with our own day and age. We, too, live in an age of unbridled lust, wicked thoughts, and violence. This fact, while terrible, ought not to come as any surprise to us, however, for the Scriptures teach us that times just as bad as the days of Noah are to return again. See Matthew 24:37; II Timothy 3:1-9; and II Peter 3:1-7. Perhaps the outbreak of sin of our day is but another sign that the coming of the Lord is near. May God grant that it may be so!

II. Preparations for the Flood (Gen. 6:13–7:9)

No attempt will be made here to try to cover everything in this section. However, certain preparations which God instructed Noah to make for the flood are to be noted.

A. The building of the ark (6:13-18). God gave Noah some rather specific instructions concerning the building of the ark. The ark was to be made of gopher wood (6:14), which is generally thought to be a species of pine, cedar, or cypress wood that could easily be worked and that would weather well. The dimensions of the ark were to be 300 cubits by 50 cubits by 30 cubits. A cubit in Bible times was a rather flexible unit of measure. However, a cubit was usually considered to be the distance from the point of a man's elbow to the tip of his middle finger, or just a trifle over 18 inches. Using this unit of measure, we come out with the dimensions of 450 x 75 x 45 feet. The ark was to have 3 decks (6:16), each was to be divided into rooms or cabins (6:14). The ark contained a door (6:16) and a window light that may have run around the entire craft from stem to stern (6:16). It should also be pointed out that the ark was probably not shaped like any modern ship today. Instead, it probably was rectangular in shape and no doubt looked much like a covered barge or flatboat.

Using the above information, some students of the Bible have attempted to figure out the approximate capacity of the ark, and the figures are almost unbelievable. If the above dimensions are correct, the ark had a total capacity of 1,500,000 cubic feet! It had a total deck area of approximately 101,250 square feet which is slightly more than the area of 20 combined standard basketball courts! And it had a displacement of over 43,000 tons which would almost make it equal in capacity to the ill-fated *Titanic* of several years ago! The sheer massiveness of such a vessel is almost enough to stagger the imagination! Little wonder that it took Noah and his sons over a century to build it!

Noah's construction of such a boat is one of the most

heroic acts of faith the world has ever seen. At the close of this chapter, the Holy Spirit records Noah's implicit obedience to God's command in these words, "Thus did Noah; according to all that God commanded him, so did he" (6:22). This verse, of course, is just a simple statement of fact, but imagine the implications of it, such as:

1. Noah may have labored *alone* much of the time. The Scriptures seem to indicate that the first of Noah's sons was not born until 20 or more years after the project was begun.

2. He labored under *discouraging circumstances.* No doubt Noah had to bear a great deal of ridicule and scorn from the world around him during those years of building and waiting.

3. He had to labor over a *long period of time.* The Bible would seem to indicate that the ark was in the process of construction for some 120 years (6:3). How many of us would have been willing to "stick to" a project like this under such circumstances? Yet in spite of these hindrances and discouraging circumstances, Noah obeyed God and in faith prepared the ark. See Hebrews 11:7 and II Peter 2:5.

B. The gathering of the animals (6:19-22; 7:2-6). Some have imagined a discrepancy between the statement made in Genesis 6:19 and the one of Genesis 7:2-3. The problem, simply stated, is that Genesis 6:19 specifies two of each kind of animal whereas Genesis 7:2-3 specifies seven of certain kinds. These verses do not contradict one another. Instead, the answer is that the instructions of Genesis 6:19 were rather general instructions which were given 120 years before the flood came. One hundred and twenty years later, as the hour of the flood approached, the additional instructions of Genesis 7:2-3 were given. Noah was not only to take a pair of each of the "unclean animals" into the ark, but a total of seven of the "clean" animals were also to be included. The reason for the increase in number of the "clean" animals was probably because they were to be used for sacrificial purposes a little later on. See Genesis 8:20.

Just how did Noah manage to get all of these beasts into

the ark? Some have imagined that Noah was a sort of primitive Frank Buck who spent years on safaries and hunting expeditions throughout the world to try to "coax" the animals into the ark. This probably was not the case at all. It is true that Genesis 6:19 says that Noah was to "bring" the animals into the ark, but Genesis 6:20, the next verse, says that they "shall come unto thee." In Genesis 7:15 the Bible gives further light on this question. There the Word says that the animals "went in unto Noah into the ark." This apparently means that the animals, by some divine compulsion, were led into the ark without any effort on Noah's part. Certainly the God who created these animals could bring this about without any difficulty. Certainly the same God who can direct ocean fish to the place of their birth and birds to their original nesting places can direct animals and birds into an ark! What a sight this must have been to see all of those animals trooping in!

C. The entering of the ark (7:1, 7-9). The invitation of the Lord contained in these verses is significant. God's gracious invitation to Noah, "Come thou and all thy house into the ark" (7:1), is the forerunner of every other gospel invitation that has ever been given. See such passages as Isaiah 66:1; Matthew 11:28-30; and Revelation 22:17 for some of the other gospel invitations of Scripture. It is also rather significant to note that Noah was not carried into the ark, nor was he compelled to go in by some outside force. Instead, he entered in of his own free will in obedient faith to the Lord. The same must also have been true of Noah's family. They, too, entered of their own free will in response to the Lord's gracious invitation. The same, of course, is still true today. Men enter the "ark of safety," the Lord Jesus Christ, of their own free choice when the invitation of the Holy Spirit is extended. How tragic that so few respond and enter.

III. The Judgment of the Flood (Gen. 7:10-24)

The meaning and implication of these verses are almost

enough to stagger the human mind. And especially is this true of verses 19 through 22 where the Bible says, "The waters prevailed exceedingly upon the earth; and all the high hills, that were under the whole heaven, were covered . . . and the mountains were covered. And all flesh died that moved upon the earth, both of fowl, and of cattle, and of beast, and of every creeping thing that creepeth upon the earth, and every man: All in whose nostrils was the breath of life, of all that was in the dry land died. . . . Noah only remained alive, and they that were with him in the ark." Who can comprehend or even begin to imagine the implications of such statements as these!

Earlier in the text (7:11), we are told that the water came from two sources. First, we are told that the "fountains of the great deep [were] broken up." This may mean that there were great underground reservoirs of water that were broken up and their waters were permitted to flow out upon the surface of the earth. Or this may mean that the waters of the sea were permitted to break their bounds and great tidal waves swept over the earth. Second, the Bible says that "the windows of heaven were opened." This may mean a great deal more than just a 40-day downpour of rain as we would know it today. Instead, this may mean that prior to the flood there was a great body of water suspended over the earth. See Genesis 1:6-7. These waters now may have been released and may have been permitted to flood the earth. If that be true, then what misery and destruction must have come upon the earth because of sin!

The question is often asked, "Was this a localized flood which involved just the immediate area of Bible lands, or was the whole earth flooded?" Bible students have been divided on this question. Some say this was a localized flood which involved just ancient Palestine and the surrounding area where men were then living. Others say that the flood waters actually covered the whole earth and as a result, life the world over was destroyed. The writer favors the latter of these two views. Those desiring to do further study on this subject will find excellent material in the book, *The Genesis Flood* by John C. Whitcomb and Henry Morris. If this view is correct, then the scientific and geologic implication of such a catastrophe would be nothing short of incomprehensible.

CONCLUSION

The account of Noah and the flood certainly ought to stand as an eternal warning to men that sin will always be punished. This is a much-needed message for our day. Yet many will not heed it. We have grown so accustomed to sin and so blind to its consequences that we will not hear and respond to such a message.

In 1952, Sir Winston Churchill, speaking about the fact that Great Britain was on the brink of bankruptcy, said that the British people had lived with danger so long that they had grown accustomed to it. He said, "I have never seen a people look better or more carefree. I wonder if they realize the treacherous trapdoor on which they stand!"

The words of Churchill certainly could be applied to our day. Many seem to feel that our world will endure indefinitely. Many feel that because life has continued without interruption for centuries that it will always do so. Nothing could be further from the truth. In fact, this is exactly the error that the Bible says men will make at the end of the age. See II Peter 3:6-7, and 10-12. Men will scoff at the idea of a God who intervenes with judgment. They will sneer at the thought of God's vengeance. But, of course, the day will come when God will again judge the earth, not with water as in the days of Noah, but with fire. Since this is true, the time to act is NOW! The time to enter God's "ark of safety" is TODAY! Enter today by receiving Christ as your Saviour and Lord!

5 Genesis 8:20–9:17

~~~~~~

A New Beginning

INTRODUCTION

STUDY GOAL

CONCLUSION

INTRODUCTION

Someone has well said that one of the most difficult things to learn to do in this life is to wait upon God. Truer words, of course, have never been spoken. In our busy world that is filled with so many activities and duties, we become accustomed to action and we like to see things move forward. Consequently, when God in His wisdom seemingly brings our little world to a standstill, we become extremely impatient; and it becomes extremely difficult for us to wait for God's time to act.

It may well be that Noah and his family were tempted to become a bit impatient with God during the days of the flood. According to the various chronological references in Genesis 6 to 8, Noah and his family remained in the ark for at least 370 days before God opened the door, and they were permitted to enter upon dry land. These may have been long wearisome days for Noah and his loved ones. In addition, we have no record anywhere in Scripture that God gave Noah any additional revelation during this extended period of time. Since this is true, one can easily understand why the 8 people in the ark might have been tempted to think that God had forgotten them. But, of course, He hadn't. The opening words of Genesis 8 read, "And God remembered Noah." This statement does not imply that God had forgotten Noah and his family and now suddenly He remembered them again. Instead, it means that the flood waters had reached their peak, and now God began to remove the waters from the earth. Just how this was done is not known. Some think that there were great earthquakes that lowered the ocean bed so as to draw the waters from the area that is now dry land. Others say that there were great climatic changes in the earth that cared for the flood waters. In any event, the waters receded, and in time Noah and his family were permitted to leave the ark and inhabit a new earth that God had cleansed from sin.

STUDY GOAL

Our study concerns those events which took place immediately following the days of the flood. It will be our purpose to examine these various events, and in so doing we hope to learn something of God's dealings with men in grace today.

I. Noah Worships (Gen. 8:20-22)

At this point in the narrative of the Book of Genesis, the flood waters receded, and Noah is ready to begin a brand new life in the new world that God has cleansed from sin. Note that the first thing that Noah did as he stepped out into the new world was worship God. This section is filled with rich spiritual truth. Two items in particular, however, are to be noted.

A. Noah's act of worship (8:20). "And Noah builded an altar unto the Lord; and took of every clean beast, and of every clean fowl, and offered burnt-offerings on the altar."

These words, of course, record Noah's simple act of worship. Some students of the Bible point out that this is the first *specific* reference to the building of an altar in the Old Testament. While this may be true, Noah's altar was not the first one ever built. Instead, in all probability God had very carefully instructed Adam and Eve in these matters shortly after their fall in the Garden of Eden. (See Gen. 3:21.) In addition, in the fourth chapter of Genesis the use of the altar is implied, though not specifically mentioned, in the story of Cain and Abel. These two references would seem to indicate that God had very carefully instructed His people concerning the need for animal sacrifice from earliest times. And now apparently Noah was simply following through, carrying out these instructions that God had given.

Just what prompted Noah's act of worship is not stated specifically in the text, but it would seem that Noah's motive was primarily one of thanksgiving to God. It probably is a mistake to say that this offering was for an atonement or a covering for sin. Noah's primary motive seemed to be one of thanksgiving. In gratitude to God for sparing their lives, Noah now expressed his thanksgiving in a visible, tangible way. God, of course, expects us to express our thanksgiving to Him today as well (see Eph. 5:20; Phil. 4:6; Col. 3:15). This is a simple truth, but many of us have forgotten it. Most of us as Christians are inclined to let our *requests* crowd out our *thanksgiving* when we pray. Consequently, many of us have been guilty of receiving much. Yet we rarely thank the Lord for His goodness.

The late Dr. Matthew Henry, author of the popular Bible commentary, made it the habit of his life that in every circumstance, whether good or bad, he would at least attempt to give thanks. On one occasion, late one night while returning home, Dr. Henry was met by a couple of thieves who relieved him of his wallet plus a few other personal possessions which he carried with him. In the light of the above statement, one could well wonder how anyone could give thanks under these circumstances. But Mr. Henry was different from some of us. Later that night as he sat by his bedside reflecting on this incident, he wrote in his diary, "The Word of God says that in everything we are to give thanks. Therefore let me be thankful in the first place that I was never robbed before. In the second place, let me be thankful that although the thieves took my wallet, they didn't take my life. In the third place, let me be thankful that although the thieves took all that I had, it wasn't very much. And finally, let me be thankful that it was I who was robbed and that it was not I who did the robbing!" Needless to say, there are few of us today who know anything at all by personal experience about this kind of gratitude. But may God help us in this ungrateful, thankless age to learn to cultivate the grace of real gratitude to God for what He is and for what He has done for us.

It is also rather interesting to see how generous Noah was in his offering. The text says he took "of *every* clean beast and of *every* clean fowl" and offered them to the Lord.

Remembering that there were only seven of each of the clean animals left on the earth, such an offering was generous indeed. Had Noah been like some Christians today, he would have reasoned, "There are only a few animals left. I had better take it easy and not overdo it. Anyway, God will certainly understand that at least my intentions are good." Not so with godly Noah. Instead, without reservations, he gave in an almost reckless manner to express his personal gratitude to God.

This thought ought to teach us that true worship and sacrificial giving are very closely related. If we are truly grateful for God's blessings, then no sacrifice will be deemed too great to make for Him. This, too, is a simple truth, but many Christians have missed it. There are many today who, when their income is reduced or there are unexpected bills to pay, will cut down first in their giving to the Lord's work. Or sometimes Christians will deny the Lord His tithe in order to make a payment on a new automobile or a new television set. Or sometimes when professing Christians begin to feel that they are becoming too busy for their own good and that some of their activities will need to be curtailed, among the first places from which they withdraw are the Sunday School and the church. Not so with Noah. Instead, Noah put God first in his life, and no sacrifice was counted too great for Him. Little wonder that his sacrifice was accepted by the Lord!

B. God's response to worship (8:21-22). "And the Lord smelled a sweet savour; and the Lord said in His heart, I will not again curse the ground any more for man's sake" (8:21).

Some liberal theologians have taken the phrase "and the Lord smelled a sweet savour" in an extremely literal sense—as though God went about sniffing the smoke that arose from Noah's altar. Such an interpretation is not only unnecessary, but it is also irreverent. Instead, the statement simply means that God saw the devotion of Noah. And so in His grace He gave the promise that He would not again curse the ground with a flood as He had done. The promise is made that as long as the earth remained, there would be "seedtime and harvest, cold and heat, summer and winter, and day and night" (8:22). These words are God's guarantee that from this point on—*until* the end of time—God will not permit such a calamity to come upon the world. This promise is still in effect today and will continue to remain in effect until in the last day when God will judge the world, not with water, but with fire (see II Peter 3:6-7, 10-13).

II. God Provided (Gen. 9:1-7)

It would appear that these seven verses look back to the creation, and in them God either renews or expands the promises He had originally given to Adam. Adam, of course, was the head of the human race. So these promises had originally been given to him. Noah, now as the head of the renewed world, receives these same promises in expanded or renewed form. Note the various provisions which the Lord made in this section.

A. The blessing of fruitfulness (9:1, 7). "And God blessed Noah . . . and said . . . Be fruitful, and multiply, and replenish the earth" (9:1).

This blessing had been originally given to Adam and Eve when they were first created (see Gen. 1:28). But now the same blessing is renewed to Noah. What all may have been involved in this command is not spelled out in any detail. However, this must mean that it is God Himself who has placed within man the mating instinct and the ability to reproduce. This truth, of course, is clearly taught elsewhere in Scripture (see Ps. 127:3). In the light of this truth, we ought, therefore, to look upon this blessing as a very sacred thing indeed.

This verse ought to remind us, also, that the Lord is the source of all spiritual fruitfulness as well. Apart from His power, we cannot produce anything of any lasting spiritual value. But with His blessing, we are able to bring forth the fruit of the Spirit (Gal. 5:22-23) and the fruit of souls (John

15:16). May the Lord enable us to so place ourselves at His disposal that He can bear His fruit in and through us.

B. The blessing of dominion (9:2). "And the fear of you and the dread of you shall be upon every beast of the earth . . . into your hand are they delivered."

The blessing of dominion over the animal kingdom was another blessing which God had originally given to Adam. In Genesis 1:28 Adam was told to "subdue" the earth and to "have dominion" over its creatures. See also Psalms 8:6-8. This blessing is now renewed to Noah. However, there does appear to be one important change. It would seem that in the dominion that God originally gave to Adam, there was nothing of fear and terror. Apparently, in the Garden of Eden earth's creatures were completely unafraid of man. But not so from the flood onward. Instead, at this point the fear and dread of man was placed into animals. And, of course, this fear and dread continues to this day. It is a well-known fact that the animal world (with the exception of a few domesticated animals) fears man. There are very few animals that will attack man unless hungry or molested. This inbred fear and dread dates back to this day when God instilled it into animals for the first time. It is also interesting to recall that the kind of dominion that Adam originally enjoyed will one day be restored during the kingdom age (see Isa. 11:6-9; Hosea 2:18).

C. The provision of food (9:3-4). "Every moving thing that liveth shall be meat for you; even as the green herb have I given you all things" (9:3).

A provision for man's diet, of course, had also been made originally back in the Garden of Eden (see Gen. 1:29). It appears, however, that God has added to His original provision. Many students of the Bible believe that man was originally a vegetarian and continued to be such until the time of the flood. But now, because climatic conditions may have changed, a different type of diet became advisable. And as a result, man is given permission to eat "every moving thing that liveth."

This verse ought also to serve as a reminder that God in His good grace has not only provided us with physical food, but He has also supplied us with the living bread which is able to satisfy our every spiritual need (see Deut. 8:3; John 6:35).

D. The provision for the sanctity of life (9:5-6). "And surely your blood of your lives will I require; at the hand of every beast will I require it, and at the hand of man; at the hand of every man's brother will I require the life of man. Whoso sheddeth man's blood, by man shall his blood be shed: for in the image of God made he man."

Most conservative students of the Bible believe that these verses are God's authorization for human government. The purpose of such a provision, of course, is obvious. According to the fourth chapter of Genesis, the first child born into the world turned out to be a murderer. He killed because he hated his fellow man. This was a dastardly act. So in order to discourage a reoccurrence of such a crime and to teach men the sacredness of human life, God authorized the institution of human government. We do not believe that these commands have ever been revoked. Instead, in the New Testament they are strongly sanctioned and even elaborated upon. See Romans 13:1-7. We believe that these verses clearly give to men the right of self-government, including the right to inflict capital punishment when necessary. Perhaps we would do well to think through these verses carefully in these days when men seem to be able to "get by" with crime and even murder with little or no protest from the government or from the public.

The implications and applications of these verses are many. But it would seem that one of the most obvious applications is that God has set a very high value upon human life. Human beings are not to be wantonly and recklessly destroyed. Instead, human life is to be respected and guarded as sacred. This high appraisal of human life is not shared by some today; and because of it, God will one day hold them accountable even though men may fail to do so. This is true, for example, of the gangster who guns down his victims for revenge, or for the sake of a few dollars, or even for the thrill of doing it. God will hold such a man responsible. The same is true of multitudes of "respectable" people who wantonly break speed laws and by so doing injure and kill their fellow men on the highways. Accidents, of course, will happen, but in most cases the slaughter on our highways is caused by carelessness, selfishness, and a reckless disregard for human life. We believe that God will hold such as these responsible for their low appraisal of the sacredness of human life.

So in this section God amply provides for man's needs. Though man had sinned and deserved nothing, provisions were made for him and a new beginning was offered.

III. God's Covenant (Gen. 9:8-17)

The word "covenant" is an important Bible word with which the student ought to become familiar. A covenant is an agreement between two parties. The covenants of the Bible are of two different kinds. Some of the covenants are *conditional*. God says, "*If you* do this, *then I* will do that." But many of the covenants of the Bible are *unconditional*. In many cases, God must have realized that man was frail and totally unable to keep his end of the bargain. So He simply unconditionally promised to do certain things. God's covenant with Noah in these verses is basically an unconditional covenant. That is, regardless of what Noah and his descendants did, God unequivocally promised that He would never again judge the world with a worldwide flood. This promise of God has never been canceled to this date. Several things are to be noted of this covenant.

A. The scope of the covenant (9:9-10). "And I, behold, I establish my covenant with you, and with your seed after you; and with every living creature that is with you."

It is rather interesting to note that God's covenant was made not only with Noah and his descendants, but its provisions were extended to the animal kingdom as well. This ought to serve as a real source of assurance to us today. If God is concerned enough about the animal kingdom to include them in His promises, then how much more must He be interested and concerned about us? This kind of logic is one that our Lord used on several occasions (see Matt. 6:26-30; 10:39-41). This is a comforting thought. Often we feel that the Lord is unaware of or unsympathetic to our need. This, of course, is not true.

B. The content of the covenant (8:21-22; 9:11). "And I will establish my covenant with you, neither shall all flesh be cut off any more by the waters of a flood; neither shall there any more be a flood to destroy the earth" (9:11).

There are two distinct clauses in the covenant agreement which God made on this occasion. Both clauses, on the surface, appear to have substantially the same meaning. But upon closer investigation there does seem to be a difference between the two. The second clause seems to be an advance upon the first. The first clause reads, "Neither shall all flesh be cut off any more by the waters of a flood." This clause might be taken to mean that future floods of gigantic proportions might come, but the entire human race would not be destroyed by them. The next clause, however, takes the thought one step further and involves an even stronger promise. God says, ". . . neither shall there any more be a flood to destroy the earth." This statement, of course, eliminates all doubt entirely. God has promised that never again will He judge the world with a flood of water to the degree that He judged the world of Noah's day. It is true that God will one day renovate the earth with fire (see II Peter 3:6-13). But never again will He drown the world with water. This promise has never been canceled and will remain uncanceled forever.

C. The sign of the covenant (9:12-17). "I do set my bow in the cloud, and it shall be for a token of a covenant between me and the earth" (9:13).

These words obviously mean that the rainbow henceforth

would be God's guarantee that He would keep His covenant. This may not mean, as some have supposed, that the rainbow did not exist before or had not been seen before. But it may mean that for the first time the rainbow was vested with meaning. Henceforth and forever, the bow would be God's reminder of His promise. Such a sign was important and necessary. Noah and his family had just lived through a horrible catastrophe and needed some sort of assurance that such a thing would not occur again. Seeing this need, God gave the sign of the bow, not to remind Himself of the promise, but to remind man that never again would the world be judged with a worldwide flood of water.

CONCLUSION

This short section, while instructive from many standpoints, is another illustration of the infinite grace of God. Adam and Eve, of course, corrupted themselves in the Garden of Eden. And following the fall, wicked men waxed worse and worse until finally God had to judge the world with a flood. At this point in history, it would have been a simple thing for God to have called it "quits" so far as His dealings with man were concerned. But not so. Instead, in infinite grace He preserved Noah and then granted him the privilege of a new and fresh beginning. God is offering something of the same opportunity to men today. For those who will enter "the ark of safety," the Lord Jesus Christ, God has promised deliverance from the flood tide of coming judgment. But not only this. In addition to deliverance from coming judgment, God also gives to men the privilege of a new life and a new beginning. He has promised to "wipe the slate clean" so far as the sin question is concerned. Then He gives to men the privilege of beginning a brand new life with Him. Such a provision is staggering to the human mind, but nonetheless true. If you have not received Christ as your Saviour and allowed Him to give you that new life, why not receive Him today?

6 Genesis 10:8-12; 11:1-9

The Building Crisis in Shinar

INTRODUCTION

STUDY GOAL

    I.   **Man's Self-Sufficiency (Gen. 10:8-12)**
        A.   Nimrod's background (10:8).
        B.   Nimrod's name (10:8).
        C.   Nimrod's vocation (10:9).
        D.   Nimrod's kingdom (10:10-12).
        E.   Nimrod's antitype.

    II.   **Man's Stubborn Rebellion (Gen. 11:1-4)**
        A.   Human life (11:1-2).
        B.   Human sin (11:3-4).

    III.   **God's Gracious Intervention (Gen. 11:5-9)**

CONCLUSION

INTRODUCTION

The material in this section marks the fourth outstanding event in the Book of Genesis. Earlier in our study we indicated that in the first eleven chapters of the book, there are four outstanding events: the Creation, the Fall, the Flood, and the Babel Crisis. The first three of these four outstanding events have already been considered in our earlier studies. And now we turn to the last of the four: namely, the account of "The Building Crisis in Shinar" as found in Genesis 10 and 11.

To the casual reader, the material in Genesis 10 and 11 may appear to be rather uninteresting reading. The two chapters include, among other things, long lists of names which give the descendants of the sons of Noah. Some have found all of this rather uninspiring. Consequently many have been tempted to skip from chapter 9 to chapter 12 in their study of the Book of Genesis, ignoring completely chapters 10 and 11. This is a mistake. It is true that these two chapters may be a little less challenging than some other parts of the book. But this does not mean that the two chapters are unimportant. To the contrary, they serve an extremely important function in the overall movement of the book. For example, these two chapters provide us with the connecting links which tie together the days of Noah with the days of Abraham. Further, these two chapters answer for us the important question as to where all the languages and nations of earth have come from. And finally, these two chapters provide us with a satisfying answer as to why God abandoned His dealings with many nations and, instead, singled out Abraham to be the father of His chosen people, Israel. These and other reasons mean that chapters 10 and 11 of Genesis are of crucial importance.

In our handling of these two chapters, we will not spend any time with the long lists of names which appear here. Instead, we will want to concentrate our attention on verses 8 to 12 of chapter 10 and verses 1 to 9 of chapter 11, which serve as parentheses in the text.

STUDY GOAL

The aim of our study will be to show that when men act in defiance of God, their best-laid plans will be frustrated and brought to naught.

I. Man's Self-Sufficiency (Gen. 10:8-12)

Every so often in the course of human history, a child will be born into the world whose life will vastly affect all men with whom he comes in contact. Sometimes such an individual will be a person of great spiritual strength and stature—a man like Enoch, Noah, Joseph, or Daniel—one who will make a great spiritual impact upon his generation. At other times, however, a child will be born into the world whose life will have an opposite effect. For example, instead of bringing blessing and strength into the lives of those around him, the life of this one may bring with it sin, wickedness, and moral degeneracy.

Nimrod, whose life story appears in these verses, was a man like this. Here was a man whose life could have been used to bring great blessing to his generation. But, unfortunately, he refused to submit himself to the Lord; and as a result, his life was used to bring about a "new low" in his day in terms of sin and rebellion against God. In this connection, several things should be noted from the text concerning this man.

A. Nimrod's background (10:8). "And Cush begat Nimrod." The first thing that we wish to observe concerning Nimrod is his background. The above text would indicate that he was the son of Cush. And according to verse 6 of this chapter, Cush was the son of Ham, that branch of Noah's family on which rested the curse of God (see Gen. 9:20-27). This statement immediately arouses our suspicions that Nimrod will be one whose life will be full of sin and rebellion against God. These suspicions will prove to be well-founded as we consider other aspects of this man's life.

B. Nimrod's name (10:8). Many students of the Bible point out to us that the name given to a child in Bible times often revealed the character and the life of that child. This, of course, is no longer true today. Today a child is given a particular name only to distinguish him from his brothers and sisters. But not so in Bible times. Instead, in Bible times the name often revealed the life and the character of the individual in question. Something of this is true of Nimrod, the man named in our text. While there are some differences of opinion on this question, many believe that the name "Nimrod" means "rebel" or more accurately "let us revolt." It would appear from this that Nimrod was a man who had a constant inner desire to revolt and rebel, and overthrow any existing order. He apparently was a rebel by nature. And this was especially true of Nimrod's attitude toward God. He was one who lived his life in open defiance against the Lord.

C. Nimrod's vocation (10:9). "He [Nimrod] was a mighty hunter before the Lord: wherefore it is said, Even as Nimrod the mighty hunter before the Lord."

It should be carefully noted here that at least twice in this verse, Nimrod is said to be a "mighty hunter before the Lord." Some have imagined that this means that Nimrod was a harmless hunter of the fields. This apparently was not the case. Instead, Nimrod was a hunter of men. The Hebrew word that is used here translated "hunter" may mean "a hero" or "a tyrant," depending on the context in which it is used. In the light of other things that appear in the context indicating that Nimrod was a rebel and a tyrant at heart, it would seem that the Holy Spirit probably intended the latter meaning. Nimrod, then, was a tyrant and a hunter of men. Perhaps he began by hunting wild animals in the field. But in time this kind of blood became too commonplace for him. So he ended up hunting and terrorizing men. A rather interesting Chaldee paraphrase of this verse which supports this interpretation reads as follows: "Cush begat Nimrod who began to prevail in wickedness, for he slew innocent blood and rebelled against Jehovah."

The phrase "before the Lord" which occurs twice in the text should also be noted. A similar expression is found in Genesis 6:11 where we are told that "the whole earth also was corrupt before God." This expression "before the Lord," then, does not mean that Nimrod's life and behavior had the Lord's approval. But it means that Nimrod was living his life in open defiance and rebellion against God. Like the infidels of past generations, Nimrod was shaking his fist in the face of Almighty God in open defiance.

D. Nimrod's kingdom (10:10-12). "And the beginning of his kingdom was Babel, and Erech, and Accad, and Calneh, in the land of Shinar. Out of that land he went forth into Assyria, and builded Nineveh, and Rehoboth-Ir, and Calah, and Resen between Nineveh and Calah [the same is the great city]" (ASV).

These verses summarize briefly Nimrod's kingdom and his empire-building program. To begin with, in verse 10 we are told that "the beginning of his kingdom was Babel." Some Bible scholars believe this means that Nimrod was the builder of ancient Babylon and that he was the leader of the building of the tower described in Genesis 11:1-9. Others feel that Nimrod merely took over the existing city of Babel and made it his kingdom after God confused the languages as recorded in Genesis 11. While some will dispute this, it appears to this author that Nimrod was directly involved in the event of Genesis 11:1-9. In fact, this author believes that it was Nimrod who led in the rebellion.

Following the building of Babel, verses 11 and 12 indicate that Nimrod continued his empire-building program. Verse 11 says, "Out of that land he went forth into Assyria, and builded Nineveh, and Rehoboth-Ir, and Calah, and Resen" (ASV). The four cities mentioned here were later amalgamated into one great city: Nineveh.

All of this building indicates once again that Nimrod's character was that of a rebel. These statements leave us with the impression that it was Nimrod's ambition to build and to establish a world empire with himself as the leader of it. If this be true, then Nimrod's plans were being carried out in open defiance of the Lord. It may well be that the Lord's original intention was that men should live simple agricultural lives. But in open defiance of God's plan, Nimrod determined to set up his own kind of kingdom.

E. **Nimrod's antitype.** Many conservative students of the Bible believe that Nimrod is a perfect forerunner of the coming Antichrist, the Man of Sin, who shall appear at the end of the age. Arthur W. Pink, in his book *Gleanings in Genesis,* has presented a rather interesting and exhaustive study of this subject. While it is not our intention to become "bogged down" at this point, the following interesting comparisons are worthy of note:

1. Nimrod's name means "the rebel." This reminds us of II Thessalonians 2:8 where the Antichrist is referred to as "the lawless one."

2. Nimrod headed up a great confederacy in open defiance against the Lord. The same will be true of the coming Antichrist. He, too, shall exalt himself and magnify himself above God (see Dan. 11:36-37).

3. Four different times in the text, the word "mighty" is used of Nimrod. Here again we are reminded that the Antichrist will come with "all power and signs and lying wonders."

4. Nimrod was a "hunter" which probably means a hunter of men. This is exactly what the Antichrist will do. Psalm 5:6 refers to him as a "bloody and a deceitful man."

5. Nimrod was a king. The Antichrist will also be a king according to Daniel 11:35.

6. Nimrod's headquarters were in Babylon. The same will be true of the coming Man of Sin. Isaiah 14:4 refers to him as the "King of Babylon," and in Revelation 17:3-5, he is associated with "mystery Babylon."

7. Nimrod's supreme desire and ambition was to make a name for himself. He had an inordinate desire for fame. The

sin of pride will also be the sin of the coming Antichrist (see II Thess. 2:4).

Whether or not Nimrod is a type of the coming Man of Sin may be debated. However, he certainly is an illustration of man's foolish attitude of self-sufficiency and independence. One has but to look about him and he will almost immediately find people even today who feel that they are entirely able to direct their own lives apart from God's help. What fools Satan has made out of many men on this point!

II. Man's Stubborn Rebellion (Gen. 11:1-4)

We turn now from the sketch of Nimrod's life to the record of his rebellious movement against God. It is true that Nimrod's name is not mentioned anywhere in chapter 11. However, it appears rather certain from the previous chapter (cf. 10:10 with 11:9) that he was the leader of the movement. Several things are to be noted from the following verses.

A. Human life (11:1-2). "And the whole earth was of one language, and of one speech. And it came to pass, as they journeyed from the east, that they found a plain in the land of Shinar; and they dwelt there."

Many students of the Bible believe that these two verses take place chronologically before the events of chapter 10. If so, perhaps these words describe the kind of life which Noah and his descendants enjoyed as well as their geographical movements following the days of the flood. What kind of lives did they live? In answer to the question, note the following:

To begin with, we are told that in those days "the whole earth was of one language and of one speech." Literally this means that the whole earth of that day was of "one lip and one word." This not only means that everyone spoke the same language, but also that their pronunciation was the same. The word "lip" emphasizes that the lips of all men were shaped alike in uttering the words. This means not only that there was one universal language used in that day, but also that the language of that day had not yet broken up into many dialects, as is true today. Just what that universal language was, no one knows. There certainly is no scriptural reason, as some have supposed, to indicate that it was Hebrew.

Further, in verse 2 we are told that the descendants of Noah "journeyed from the east" and "found a plain in the land of Shinar and they dwelt there." Some have imagined that there was something inherently sinful about the movement to this new location. This may not have been the case. The descendants of Noah may have lived an agricultural or nomadic life which may have demanded a great deal of moving from place to place. And perhaps in the natural course of their journeyings, they eventually came to the plain of Shinar. Since the plain of Shinar was a fertile spot, it is not too surprising to read that they "dwelt there." While some will dispute this, it appears that the moves made by the descendants of Noah up to this point were completely innocent. Up to this point, they may not have had even the thought of rebelling against God. Such a thought did come later in the course of time, and because of it God had to bring judgment on this generation.

B. Human sin (11:3-4). "And they said one to another, Go to, let us make brick, and burn them throughly. And they had brick for stone, and slime had they for mortar. And they said, Go to, let us build us a city and a tower, whose top may reach unto heaven; and let us make a name, lest we be scattered abroad upon the face of the whole earth."

While the lives and the moves made by the descendants of Noah may have been innocent during the period of time described in the first two verses of the chapter, they did not remain innocent and free from sin. Instead, some time after—and no one can say how long after—they began to conceive the idea of building a city and a tower in blatant defiance of God. So the building boom began. Our text says that they used brick for stone, and slime (or bitumen) for mortar. Ordinary houses in Babylon were almost always built of bricks of this kind which probably were made out of sun-dried clay. In this part of the world, there are very few stones that are suitable for building purposes. But the plain of Shinar abounds with a heavy rich clay which can be made into brick. Temperatures in this part of the world rise as high as 115 degrees Fahrenheit. At such temperatures, clay will harden into brick suitable for building in a matter of two or three days. However, these builders were not content with just sun-dried brick. Instead, their bricks were kiln-dried which made them as hard as stone. This certainly would indicate the seriousness of the venture which they were undertaking.

Just what this tower may have looked like is open to question. Bible archeologists have found the remains of several towers in the area of ancient Babylon. One of these may be the original tower of Genesis 11, or all of them may be replicas of the original one. These Babylonian towers were called *ziggurats* and followed the same basic style of architecture. The base was square. On top of this square base were built receding layers. And on the top there was usually erected an altar to some pagan god. Whether the original tower of Genesis 11 resembled such a construction, no one knows. But it is highly probable that it did. Many have wondered about the statement of verse 4, where we are told that Nimrod and his followers desired to build a tower "whose top may reach unto heaven." Is this just a figure of speech, or did these Shinar builders actually think that such a thing could be done? It is the opinion of this writer that this is not just a figure of speech. Instead, so great was their pride and so blatant was their defiance of God that they foolishly supposed that such a thing could be done. Historians tell us that both the Babylonians and Assyrians greatly prided themselves on the height of their temples and boasted that their tops reached to the very heavens. Such pride and boasting must have also been in the minds of Nimrod and his followers.

What was the purpose behind such a project? Verse 4 answers the question. Here we hear Nimrod and his followers say, "Let us make us a name, lest we be scattered abroad upon the face of the whole earth." Some have supposed that the city and tower of the Shinar builders was being constructed as a place of security against a second flood. This hardly seems likely. Instead, the motive seems to have been a double one: pride and defiance of God. First, the motive was that of pride. Note carefully the occurrence of the phrase "Let *us*." Also note the phrase, "Let us make *a name for ourselves*." There was no thought of God and His will in the minds of Nimrod and his followers. Instead, they were filled with pride and self-will. And then second, the motive of Nimrod and his followers was that of blatant defiance of God. Earlier, in Genesis 9:1, God had said, "Be fruitful and multiply and replenish the earth." Such a command, of course, involved scattering out and spreading abroad. Upon hearing such a command, Nimrod and his followers may have felt that such a command would destroy their inner unity and would leave them unsafe and unprotected from their enemies. So, rather than obey God—in rebellion against His will, they chose to remain a closely welded unit; and the tower became a symbol of their defiance.

As God looks at the world today, He still sees an attitude similar to that of Nimrod and the tower of Babel. He sees men whose hearts are filled with pride and self-will. And He still sees those who in rebellion choose to ignore God and seek to run their own lives. Such an attitude is not only seen in the lives of the unsaved, but unfortunately, it is also seen on occasion in the lives of those who profess His name.

III. God's Gracious Intervention (Gen. 11:5-9)

Just how long the people of Babel worked on their city and tower is not stated specifically in this chapter. The implication of the text, however, seems to be that they had not been building very long when God graciously intervened. God must have realized that if He permitted Nimrod's project to go on, the power of sin would grow and the pride of man would become more open and blatant. So he graciously stepped into the picture and brought the building project to a halt.

Just how God brought this building to a halt is open to question. Verse 7 says that God "confounded" their language. But just how this was accomplished is not stated. Some contend that God wrought upon the ears of these men so that they were unable to understand one another. Others say that God judged these men by touching their lips so that they could no longer speak intelligently to one another. Still others say that God hastened man's natural tendency to form different dialects, and on this basis the building boom in Shinar came to an end. Perhaps it is just enough to know that God stepped into this scene—and whatever device He used was sufficient to bring this expression of man's pride and defiance to an end.

CONCLUSION

The story of the building crisis in Shinar is but an illustration of the heart attitude that sinful man has always taken toward God. Man today would still rather have his own way than submit to the lordship of Christ. What does God see when He looks into your heart, my friend? How are you building the "tower" of your life? Do your plans, ambitions, and use of time, talent, and material things take God into account? Or is your attitude similar to that of Nimrod and his followers? If God is to be pleased, and if our lives are to be lived to the fullest, then God and His will must be central. We must surrender every area of life to Him and obey His will implicitly. Only then will our lives prove to be truly useful and happy. Fully yield your life to Him today.

7 Genesis 12:1-9

The Call of Abram

INTRODUCTION

STUDY GOAL

CONCLUSION

INTRODUCTION

The material in this section marks an important turning point in the overall movement of the Book of Genesis. As indicated in our earlier studies, the Book of Genesis is clearly divided into two major divisions. In chapters 1 to 11, the first major division, there are *four outstanding events*: the Creation, the Fall, the Flood, and the Babel Crisis. Beginning with chapter 12, however, a second major division of the book is begun and continues to the end of the book. In this second main division, chapters 12 to 50, the author deals with *four outstanding characters*: Abraham, Isaac, Jacob, and Joseph. Having considered the various events contained in the first main division, we turn now to a study of the first of four outstanding characters: Abraham, the man of faith.

The importance of Abraham, so far as the Biblical record is concerned, can scarcely be overemphasized. Consider, for example, the place of prominence that is given to this man in the Word of God. The first 2,000 years (and probably more) of human history are all covered in 11 chapters of the Bible (Gen. 1-11). No less than 20 generations are covered in these 11 chapters. Chapter 12 begins the record of Abraham's life; and from this point onward, the Holy Spirit's pace of the record of human history slows down considerably and centers largely on this one man, Abraham. Chapters 12 to 50 of Genesis, for example, cover only a period of about 400 years and are devoted entirely to the history of Abraham and three of his descendants—Isaac, Jacob, and Joseph. The rest of the Old Testament deals with the history of the nation which sprang from Abraham; that is, the nation of Israel. And finally, all of the rest of the Bible is occupied with and centers on Abraham's greater Son, the Lord Jesus Christ. All of this is simply an indication that Abraham holds an important strategic place in the Word of God and in God's wonderful plan of redemption. Careful consideration, therefore, needs to be given to this important man of history.

In our study of the Book of Genesis, three chapters will be

devoted to the story of Abraham's life. The first study will be concerned with his call. A second study will deal with some of the promises made to him. And finally, a third and final study will be concentrated on the testings of Abraham. While many things of necessity will need to be left out of the story of Abraham because of the brevity of time, it is hoped that these three lessons will serve as a brief summary of his life and place in God's program.

STUDY GOAL

The aim of our study for today is to show how God uses men to bring about His purposes, and to show the importance of faith and complete obedience to His will for our lives.

I. Abram's Call (Gen. 12:1)

"Now the Lord had said unto Abram, Get thee out of thy country, and from thy kindred, and from thy father's house, unto a land that I will shew thee."

This text absolutely abounds with teaching truth. In fact, the careful student of the Word could, without any difficulty, spend days on this one verse alone without even beginning to exhaust its contents. Only a few of the more important facts, however, will be noted from the text relative to Abram's call.

A. The source of the call (12:1). "Now the Lord had said unto Abram, Get thee out of thy country." The source of Abram's call, of course, is suggested by the first five words of the text, "Now the Lord had said." It was God Himself who took the initiative in Abram's life. It was not Abram who made the first move toward God. Instead, it was God who simply broke into Abram's life, and it was He who took the steps necessary to bring this man to Himself.

In this connection, it is rather interesting to note the kind of life that Abram was living when God called him. Joshua 24:2 gives us a bit of insight on this question. There Joshua, speaking of Israel, says, "Thus saith the Lord God of Israel,

Your fathers dwelt on the other side of the flood in old time, even Terah, the father of Abraham, and the father of Nachor: and *they served other gods.*" It would appear from this verse that when the call of God came, Abram was a heathen idolater. He was not a worshiper of the true and living God. Instead, he was living in a pagan country and in a pagan home and was a worshiper of pagan, false gods. In recent years it has been learned that Ur of the Chaldees, Abram's home town, was the center of worship for the moon god, Nanna. Doubtless, Abram was a worshiper of this false god prior to the call of the Lord upon his life.

We call attention to all of this because the story of Abram's call is a beautiful picture of God's dealings with men today. When the call of God came, Abram was living in a pagan land, alienated from God, a stranger to the promises of God, living under judgment, and doomed to destruction. Yet God simply broke into this man's life and called Abram to Himself. So it is with every child of God today. By our first birth, we are alienated from God, are living under the judgment of hell, and are doomed to everlasting judgment. Yet in grace God breaks into our lives and calls us to Himself. (See Eph. 2:11-13; Rom. 8:30.)

B. The demands of the call (12:1). "Get thee out of thy country, and from thy kindred, and from thy father's house." Someone has observed that the call of God is *always* away from the world, away from sin, and away from the old life of wickedness. This truth is graphically illustrated in the life of Abram. Here we are told of three things which Abram was to leave.

1. First, Abram was to leave his *country.* For him this meant the severance of literal, physical, and geographical ties. Such a demand certainly was not an easy one to obey. Ur of the Chaldees was one of the great cities of the Mesopotamian plain. It was a prosperous city of high culture. Recent studies have revealed that the average middle class home in Ur had from 10 to 20 rooms along with adequate quarters for

servants. Children in ancient Ur were taught reading, writing, and arithmetic. They solved problems in square and cube roots. The city of Ur itself was a city of commerce, trade, and a prosperous economy. All of this, of course, would make Ur a comfortable and desirable place in which to live. Yet God called His man away from all this. Henceforth Abram was to be a stranger and a pilgrim in the earth with no certain dwelling place.

Sometimes for the child of God today such a literal departure from one's own country is involved in God's call. This certainly would be true of the missionary who is called to the foreign mission field. Like Abram of old, the modern missionary knows what it means to leave country and homeland behind to go into a strange land. While God may not always call all of us out of our countries and homelands in quite this literal a fashion today, the principle certainly holds true in a spiritual way. The call of God is *always* away from sin and involves a complete break with the old life.

2. Secondly, Abram was to leave his *kindred*. It is generally thought that the term "kindred" is a rather general term referring to Abram's relatives, including the family of Nahor and Haran (see 11:26). In this statement, the call of God becomes a little more demanding. No family interest is to come between him and the will of God.

3. Finally, Abram was to leave his *father's house*. In this statement, of course, the call of God reaches its most demanding proportions. Abram was not to allow even the members of his immediate family circle to stand in his way. Instead, he was to turn his back upon every earthly tie which he possessed. It is rather interesting to note now that it was in this third area that Abram had some difficulty. Back in Genesis 11:31 we learn that Abram started out for Canaan, the promised land of blessing. But he was accompanied by Terah, his father, and by Lot, his nephew. It would appear that this was an act of incomplete obedience on Abram's part. God told him to sever his ties completely. Yet Abram compromised by taking with him at least two members of his

family.

What a picture this is of many Christians today who start out with real enthusiasm in the Christian life, yet whose effectiveness is nullified because of only partial obedience. Abram, of course, paid dearly for his act. Genesis 11:31 says that Abram journeyed only as far as Haran where he dwelt for about six years. The name "Haran" means "dry" or "parched" or "fruitless." These terms certainly are characteristic of Abram's life during those six years. For all practical purposes, these were wasted years. There is no record that Abram built any altars here or that he prayed. There is no record of any revelations or encouragements from the Lord, no appearances, no victory, no progress, no growth. Instead, these were totally barren years until God once again stepped into the picture and removed the hindering cause by taking the life of Terah (11:32). As a result Abram is finally brought back to the place of blessing again. How typical this is of the barren lives of so many Christians today because of incomplete obedience to the will of God! And how sad that God must deal with us in judgment before we will begin to obey!

The call of God upon Abram's life was extremely severe in its demands. Not one single thing was to stand in Abram's way. Instead, he was to turn his back upon every earthly tie he had ever known. The demands of discipleship are no less demanding today. Instead, if we are to experience His blessing, we must turn to Him in unreserved obedience, leaving behind all that hinders us. (See Matt. 10:37-39.)

C. The direction of the call (12:1). ". . . unto a land that I will show thee." It is important that we observe that the call of God had not only a negative side to it, but also a positive side. Abram was not only to separate himself *from* certain things, but he was also to cleave *unto* certain other things that God would now show to him. God not only called Abram *out of* the old life, but He also called him *unto* a land. So it is with the Christian today. The child of God is not to separate himself from sin and the world simply for the sake of separating himself. Instead, separation has a positive side to it as well as a negative one. We are not only to renounce the world, but we are also to cleave to the Lord and to His Word, and we are to seek after those things that are a part of that "better land." How sad that many Christians know only the negative side of this truth. They "don't do this and they don't do that," which is right and proper. Yet they know little or nothing at all about a positive submission and obedience to the Lord.

II. God's Promises (Gen. 12:2-3)

In the previous section, we noted that Abram was called upon by God to make a threefold sacrifice. He was to leave country and kindred and father's house. In the section before us now, we will see how any sacrifices which Abram may have made were more than compensated for by God's promise of blessings. In these two verses, a threefold promise is made. The promise involved, among other things, a land, a seed, and a blessing. As we shall discover in our later studies, the entire life story of Abram may be gathered about these three important promises. Several items should be noted concerning each of these three promises.

A. A land (12:1). God's promise of a land is actually found at the close of verse 1 where God promises, "Get thee out of thy country . . . *unto a land* that I will shew thee." The land referred to here, of course, is the land of Palestine. And the meaning of the promise is that this land was to belong to Abram and his descendants. While the promise of the land is just briefly referred to here, this part of the covenant is spelled out in much greater detail in some of the later appearances which God made to Abram. See Genesis 13:14-15; 15:18-21 (in this passage the exact dimensions of the land are given); 17:8 (note here that God adds one further detail. The land is to be for an "everlasting possession" to Abram and his seed after him).

Some have scoffed at this promise pointing out that until

the day of his death, Abram never possessed more than a burial plot in the land of Palestine that he could legally call his own (see Gen. 23:19). So Abram died without ever having this promise fulfilled to him personally and literally. Does this mean that God's promise was worthless and meaningless? Not at all. Whereas it is true that Abram may not have seen a personal and literal fulfillment of this promise in his lifetime, in later years this land which God promised to Abram did become the possession of his descendants. And in a more complete way, we believe that this promise will have its fullest and most complete fulfillment at the end of the age during the millennial reign of Christ when the land of Canaan will be given once again to the nation of Israel, the descendants of Abram (see Amos 9:15).

It is true that if this life were all, we would have to say that God had failed Abram. But this life is by no means the whole story. God is not limited to just this life in fulfilling His promises. Instead, in some cases we must wait until that day when we shall be with Him before we understand all things fully and completely. We believe this will be true of Abram and God's promise of the land. The day will yet come when this promise will be kept implicitly (see Heb. 11:13).

B. A seed (12:2). God's promise of the seed is contained in the opening words of verse 2 where God says, "And I will make of thee *a great nation.*" Involved in these few brief words is the promise of a seed. In our later studies, we will discover that Abram was sorely tried by God with respect to this second promise. Yet we believe that this promise was fulfilled in at least three distinct ways.

1. To begin with, God kept His promise of a seed in the giving of Isaac, and in time the descendants of Abram did become a great nation. Under David and Solomon, Israel became one of the greatest nations on the face of the earth. This promise may also look forward to the end of the age when the nation of Israel, the physical descendants of Abram, will once again be restored to a place of prominence among the nations of earth. And in that day Abram and his

descendants shall indeed become "a great nation."

2. But God's promise of a "seed," we believe, was fulfilled in a second way. According to the New Testament, this promise of a "seed" refers not only to the physical descendants of Abram, but it also refers to the Lord Jesus Christ Himself. According to Galatians 3:16, Christ Himself is said to be the "seed" of Abraham.

3. Finally, we believe that this promise of a "seed" also has as its fulfillment all who share Abram's faith. Galatians 3:29 indicates that all who are in Christ and who share Abram's faith are his spiritual seed. In these various ways, God did, and is continuing to, keep His promise to Abram concerning the seed.

C. A blessing (12:2-3). God's third promise, of a blessing, is contained in the closing words of verse 2 as well as in verse 3 where God said, "And I will bless thee, and make thy name great; and thou shalt be a blessing: And I will bless them that bless thee, and curse him that curseth thee: and in thee shall all families of the earth be blessed." In our later studies, we will discover that God sorely tried Abram with respect to this promise as well. And yet, in spite of the trials, God once again kept His promise to Abram. Abram, without question, was one of the greatest and most important men of all history. He is revered today by Jews, Moslems, and Christians alike. Beyond this, Abram's life has proved to be a blessing in a more complete way, for through him the Lord Jesus Christ, Abram's greater Son, eventually came into the world. And, of course, because of the coming of Abraham's greater seed, the Lord Jesus Christ, all of the families of the earth have been blessed throughout the ages of eternity.

These two verses certainly abound with the precious promises of God. And of course, God did not break His promises to Abram. Instead, they have been fulfilled and are continuing to be fulfilled even today. This ought to serve as a real means of assurance to us today, enabling us to cling to Him for our every need. The same God who promised Abram His blessing is alive today. Let us just learn, as did Abram, that God's promises, though sometimes delayed, will never fail. God always keeps His Word.

III. Abram's Obedience (Gen. 12:4-9)

While there is a great deal of truth contained in these verses, the central thought is the fact of Abram's obedience to the will of God. This obedience is briefly summarized in the words of verse 4 where the Holy Spirit says, "So Abram departed, as the Lord had spoken unto him. . . . and Abram was seventy and five years old when he departed out of Haran."

Some have had difficulty reconciling this verse with a statement made by Stephen concerning Abraham in his sermon of Acts 7. In Acts 7:2 Stephen says that God called Abraham while "he was in Mesopotamia, before he dwelt at Charran [Haran]." Yet Genesis 12:4 seems to imply that the call of God came while Abram was dwelling at Haran. It would seem to this author that there were probably two different calls that were issued by the Lord. First, the call of God came while Abram was dwelling at Ur. Abram, however, only partially obeyed this call. He took with him members of his family, which had been expressly forbidden by the Lord, and went only as far as Haran. Abram remained at Haran for a time and perhaps began to settle down there to the point where the call of God was all but forgotten. As a result, God once again moved in the heart of Abram and renewed the call. And this time Abram obeyed implicitly.

If all of this be true, then what a contrast there is here between Genesis 11:31 and Genesis 12:4! The first verse tells of incomplete obedience to the will of God. The second verse tells of full surrender. The first tells of partial obedience and wasted years. The second tells of full obedience and resulting blessing. The two verses, of course, simply mean that the time eventually came when Abram broke his ties completely with the old life. He turned his back and left behind him all of the scenes that were familiar to him. And in implicit obedience, he moved forward trusting God to lead him. The Book of Hebrews immortalizes this act, indicating that it was by *faith* that Abram obeyed (see Heb. 11:8). Many of Abram's later acts were performed by faith, but this was his first great act of faith. He broke his ties completely with his former life and began the long, narrow journey that leads from earth to heaven.

CONCLUSION

The call of God upon Abram's life is basically the same call that God extends to men today. God called Abram to separate himself from his family, his friends, and his familiar surroundings. To go where God wants us to go and to be what God wants us to be requires the same kind of obedience and submission today. Obedience to the will of God often demands that we be willing to separate ourselves from our families, our familiar surroundings, and from certain natural desires and ambitions. May God help us to turn our backs upon all that is necessary in order that we may serve Him well.

8 Genesis 17:1-8, 15-22

The Promised Son

INTRODUCTION

STUDY GOAL

CONCLUSION

INTRODUCTION

Someone has well said that faith that is never tested will never grow strong. This statement certainly is one of the fundamental laws of the Christian life, and it can be illustrated in many different ways. For example, steel must be tempered with fire in order to become keen. Gold must be purified by passing through fire before it becomes useful. Silver must be constantly polished if it is to remain clean and bright. The soil must be plowed and broken before it will bring forth fruit. In like manner, the believer needs to be constantly tested and tried if he is to grow strong in faith and if he is to become a fruitful Christian.

The life of Abraham is a perfect illustration of this truth, for this man was tested and tried as perhaps no other man in history. For example, in our previous lesson we learned that the Abrahamic covenant given in Genesis 12 centered around three important promises. First, God promised Abram the *land* of Canaan extending from the river of Egypt to the Euphrates River. Secondly, involved in the covenant was the promise of a *blessing*. Abram was to be a blessing to all the families of earth. And finally, at the very heart of the covenant, was the promise of a *seed*. Now, concerning each of these three promises Abram was severely tested and tried.

Note, for example, how Abram was tried with respect to the third of these three promises—the promise of a seed. To begin with, there may have been a time when Abram centered his hopes for a promised heir in his nephew Lot. In Genesis 11:30 and 31 we read that "Sarai was barren; she had no child. . . . and they went forth with them from Ur of the Chaldees, to go into the land of Canaan." "Terah took Abram his son and Lot the son of Haran his son's son." Whereas it is true that the Holy Spirit does not say explicitly that Abram had centered his hopes in Lot, the fact that Sarai is declared to be barren and that Lot is included in the group may suggest that there was a time when Abram was thinking of Lot as the promised heir. But, of course, the time came when God made it clear to Abram that Lot was not the heir. Further, there was a time when Abram had centered his hopes for an heir in his servant Eliezer. In Genesis 15:2 we read, "And Abram said, Lord God, what wilt thou give me, seeing I go childless, and the steward of my house is this Eliezer of Damascus?" The implication of this statement is that at this point Abram was ready to accept Eliezer as his heir. But God made it clear that Eliezer was not the heir, and Abram was forced to walk by faith alone. Finally, some 10 years later we learn that Abram again was ready to settle for an earthly substitute instead of the promised seed. In Genesis 16 we read the story of the birth of Ishmael, Abram's son by Sarai's handmaid, Hagar. The story of Genesis 16 is one of the saddest stories of the Old Testament, for it indicates that Abram, in a moment of impatience, weakness, and doubt, was ready to fulfill the promise of a seed in his own way. So God tested and tried Abram over and over again with respect to this promise of a seed. In fact, for some 25 years (cf. Gen. 12:4 with 17:17) God tested this man on this point to help him to walk by faith.

In the chapter before us, after years of testing, God is now about ready to keep His promise to Abram concerning the seed. After 25 years of waiting, Abram is about to see the fulfillment of God's promise. In our handling of the chapter, we will not be dealing with all of it. Instead, we will consider but two paragraphs of the chapter: verses 1 to 8 where God's promise is confirmed, and verses 15 to 22 where God's promise is completed.

STUDY GOAL

The purpose of this study is to show that God's promises are always fulfilled in His time and way, and that God's testings are designed to lead us to the point of uncompromising submission to His will for our lives.

I. God's Promise Confirmed (Gen. 17:1-8)

It is rather interesting to observe that the word "covenant" is used some 13 different times in this chapter. The covenant that is referred to here, however, is not a new one. Instead, the covenant of this chapter is only the confirmation of one that had been made years earlier. God's original promise had been given in Genesis 12:1 to 3, the passage studied in an earlier lesson. The Lord, however, appeared to Abram several times after the experience of Genesis 12, either to confirm or to add to the covenant. In fact, the appearance of the Lord to Abram here in Genesis 17 is the fifth time that God appeared to him to spell out the details of the agreement. See Genesis 12:1-3; 12:7; 13:14-18; and 15:1-21 for the previous appearances. The purpose of these various appearances, as indicated, was either to confirm or to add new details to the already existing agreement. Now, in chapter 17 the promise of God reaches its fullest proportion. We will now want to give ourselves to a study of the various details of the promise.

A. The time (17:1). "And when Abram was ninety years old and nine, the Lord appeared unto Abram."

It should be carefully noted that Abram was 75 years old when he left Haran to go into the land of Canaan (see Gen. 12:4). He was 86 years old when Ishmael was born to him from Hagar (see Gen. 16:16). And now, here in the opening words of chapter 17, we learn that Abram was 99 years of age when the Lord again appeared. It seems rather significant to this author that a period of at least 13 years elapsed between Genesis 16 and Genesis 17, and nowhere in Scripture do we have a record of any of the events of these years, nor do we have anywhere the record of a message which God spoke during this period of time. In contrast, we do have a great deal of information concerning the events that took place between the time Abram left Haran and the time that Ishmael was born. All of chapters 12 to 16 are a description of these years. However, the Scriptures are strangely silent concerning the period between the birth of Ishmael and the appearance of God, recorded in Genesis 17. Instead, the Holy Spirit passes over it without comment. Immediately we ask, "Why this obvious silence?" Could it be that the Holy Spirit is purposely silent concerning these years in order to teach us that these were wasted years or years of spiritual barrenness brought on because of Abram's impatience? Years before, God had promised Abram a seed. But the years passed by and there was no answer from God. And as a result, Abram decided to take matters into his own hands instead of waiting on God. So Ishmael was born to Abram by Sarai's handmaid, Hagar. It is the opinion of this author that God was displeased with this act of impatience, and so for 13 long years, God was silent, and the years passed by with no message from Him.

What a warning this should be to us today. When we sin or become impatient with God, we, too, like Abram, lose something. We do not lose our salvation, thank God, but we do lose the joy of our fellowship with Him. Our joy is gone, our peace is gone, we can no longer pray as we once did, we no longer are conscious of the Lord's presence with us, and in general we live lives that are wasted and empty. Doubtless Abram experienced 13 years of this kind of wasted existence because of the impatient act of Genesis 16.

It should be noted, however, that now after 13 years of barrenness, God once again made a move in Abram's direction to affect a reconciliation between Himself and His man. This move of God is typical of God's ways. As learned earlier, it is always God who makes the first move toward sinful man to bring the sinner to Himself. For example, it was God who made the first move toward sinful man in the Garden of Eden. Again, it was God who made the first move toward Abram in Genesis 12 while he was still an idolater in Ur of the Chaldees. And now once again in this chapter, it is God who makes the first move toward disobedient Abram to bring about a reconciliation. What a thrilling illustration this is of the sovereign grace of God!

B. The author (17:1). "And when Abram was ninety years old and nine, the Lord appeared to Abram, and said unto him, *I am the Almighty God.*"

The name "Almighty God" is the name *El Shaddai* in the language of the Old Testament. This name is found 6 times in the Book of Genesis and 31 times in the Book of Job. However, since this is its first occurrence in the Word of God, a brief word of comment is in order. The name *Shaddai* comes from a root which means "to deal violently," and in reference to God, this name would mean "to be powerful" or "to be strong." Or perhaps the name could be translated as "the All-sufficient God." If this be true, then this name has real meaning in this passage. Recall that by this time, it was impossible for either Abram or Sarai to produce an heir. Their case was hopeless. In fact, the Book of Romans says that their bodies were "as good as dead" so far as this physical function was concerned (see Rom. 4:19). Yet in the face of this seemingly impossible dilemma, God now was revealing Himself as *El Shaddai,* the All-powerful or All-sufficient God. God was now going to demonstrate to Abram that He was able to compel even nature to do that which was absolutely contrary to itself in order that His sovereign purpose might be fulfilled.

It may be that there is just a slight touch of rebuke in these words as well. In effect, God is saying to Abram, "Abram, I am the Almighty God, the All-powerful God. I am *El Shaddai.* You have tried by unlawful means and have failed. Now leave it all to Me and I will do it My way. The seed and the inheritance and everything related to it will be everlastingly settled now, for I am about to demonstrate My power. I am the Almighty!" That this touch of rebuke must have been in the mind of the Lord is further demonstrated in the closing words of verse 1 where we read of Abram's obligation to the promise of God.

C. The obligation (17:1). "The Lord appeared to Abram, and said unto him, I am the Almighty God; *walk before me, and be thou perfect.*"

The expression "walk before me" is an interesting one and highly suggestive. The picture is that of a child who runs ahead and plays while his father follows along behind a short distance away. The child has no fear because he is perfectly assured that his father is right behind and sufficient to meet any emergency that may arise. To walk before God in a spiritual way would mean that we are to *think,* and *act,* and *speak,* and *walk* as though we were in His presence and dwelling under His watchful eye at all times. Once again, there is a touch of rebuke in these words. In effect, God is saying, "Abram, in past days you have been content to dwell out of reach of my watch-care and blessing. You have not been walking in fellowship with Me. Now, I want you to walk before Me in truth, and I want you to be absolutely obedient to My Word."

It is rather interesting to observe how Abram responded to this rebuke. In verse 3 we read, "And Abram fell on his face." Without question this was not only an act of worship on Abram's part, but also, there was confession and repentance involved here. Realizing how impatient and unfaithful he had been, Abram fell upon his face in the dust in sincere repentance and confession of sin.

D. The encouragement (17:5). "Neither shall thy name any more be called Abram, but thy name shall be Abraham; for a father of many nations have I made thee."

There is a good deal of mystery which shrouds the changing of Abram's name and it may be that we will never know the complete answer as to the purpose for this act. There is, however, a rather interesting parallel in the Scriptures involving a grandson of Abraham: namely, Jacob the supplanter. Recall the contents of Genesis 32 where we read the story of God wrestling with Jacob. Jacob's name of course, meant "supplanter," and in that chapter we read how God wrestled with him until Jacob surrendered, and God changed his name to "Israel" meaning "The Prince of God." This story has often been used as an illustration of men wrestling with God in prayer, but note carefully that it was God who wrestled and not Jacob. The teaching of Genesis 32 is that God was wrestling with Jacob in an effort to subdue his stubborn self-will and to bring this man to the point of submission and complete obedience. If this be true, then perhaps we have a parallel in Genesis 17. Abram's name means "high father," and now it was being changed to "Abraham" which means, "father of a multitude." Perhaps the change in the name is an indication that Abraham, like his grandson Jacob, repented sincerely of his sin and submitted himself fully to the will of God. And in token of this kind of submission, God changed his name from "Abram" to "Abraham."

E. The renewed blessing (17:2, 6-8). As indicated earlier, the covenant of this chapter is not a new one. Instead, it is only the confirmation of a promise that had been made years earlier. In these verses, no blessings are promised to Abraham that had not been promised before, but the emphasis does seem to be upon the divine Source from which these blessings were to come. Note the seven "I wills" of this section:

1. "*I will* make my covenant between me and thee" (v. 21).

2. "*I will* multiply thee exeedingly" (v. 2).

3. "*I will* make thee exceeding fruitful" (v. 6).

4. "*I will* make nations of thee, and kings shall come out of thee" (v. 6).

5. "*I will* establish my covenant between me . . . and thy seed . . . for an everlasting covenant" (v. 7).

6. "*I will* give . . . thy seed . . . all the land of Canaan" (v. 8).

7. "*I will* be their God" (v. 8).

In effect God is saying, "Abraham, you've tried in your way and have failed. Now, stand still and see the salvation of the Lord. What you could never do by the work of the flesh, now I will do by My grace and by My mighty power!" What a rebuke this was, and yet what a gracious promise on the part of the Lord!

II. The Promise Completed (Gen. 17:15-22)

God's original promise to Abraham had been made in Genesis 12:1 to 3. However, many of the details of that original promise were not spelled out until years later. This is especially true of God's promise of a seed. In Genesis 12:1 God had promised Abraham a seed when He said, "I will make of thee a great nation." However, for some 25 years, God withheld many of the details as to just how this promise would be fulfilled. In the verses before us, God now completed the details of this promise of a seed. Two important details are to be noted in our study.

A. The inclusion of Sarah (17:15-16). "And God said unto Abraham, As for Sarai thy wife, thou shalt not call her name Sarai, but Sarah shall her name be. And I will bless her, and give thee a son of her."

The inclusion of Sarai in the plan of God is a highly important detail, for prior to this there had been no word from God to indicate that she would actually be the mother of the long-promised seed. But now the word is given. Sarai is to be the mother of the promised seed; and in token of this, her name is changed from "Sarai" to "Sarah."

Earlier we noted that the changing of Abraham's name indicated a new act of submission and obedience to the will of the Lord. In the light of this fact, could it be possible that the changing of Sarai's name also indicates a new attitude of submission and devotion on her part? An interesting passage in this connection is Hebrews 11:11 where we read, "*Through faith* also Sara herself received strength to conceive seed, and was delivered of a child when she was past age, *because she judged him faithful who had promised.*" It seems rather obvious from this passage that a change did take place in Sarai's heart, and in token of it God changed her name from Sarai meaning "princely" to Sarah meaning "The princess of God."

Perhaps of even greater importance is the second detail that God was adding to His promise. Sarah was not only to be included, but Ishmael was to be excluded.

B. The exclusion of Ishmael (17:17-22). It is rather interesting to observe from these verses Abraham's *immediate* response to God's promise concerning the inclusion of Sarah. In verses 17 and 18 we are told that there was a twofold response. To begin with, there was an *inner response*. In verse 17 we read that Abraham fell on his face in what may have been a pretense at worship, but in his heart he laughed. Some have sought to defend Abraham in this. But it seems perfectly clear that this was nothing other than an act of unbelief. Abraham had real difficulty even at this point in believing that such a thing could be. And so in the secret of his own heart he laughed at the promises of God. But there was also an *outward* response from Abraham. What he felt in his heart could not be concealed. So in verse 18 we hear him say, "O that Ishmael might live before thee!" On the surface these words may sound very devout, but they were actually an expression of unbelief. In essence, Abraham was saying, "God, here's Ishmael. Let's be satisfied with him!" This was a terrible statement for Abraham to make, for Ishmael was something of a memorial to Abraham's failure and impatience. Yet Abraham sought to please God by offering him this earthly substitute. God's answer to such a suggestion must have sounded devastating to Abraham. We read it in verses 19 to 21, "And God said, Sarah thy wife shall bear thee a son indeed; and thou shalt call his name Isaac. . . . And as for Ishmael, I have heard thee . . . and I will make him a great nation. But my covenant will I establish with Isaac, which Sarah shall bear unto thee at this set time in the next year."

It would almost appear as if God was pulling out all of the props from underneath Abraham with these words, leaving him no alternative but to walk by faith. The story, of course, does not end here. The circumcision of Abraham and his household recorded in the later verses of this chapter is an indication that from this point onward, Abraham began to walk in faith with an eye single to the purposes of God until the day that Isaac was born (see Rom. 4:19-21). At last faith was triumphant. There were no more doubts and misgivings from this point on. Instead Abraham submitted completely.

CONCLUSION

The trials of Abraham are but an illustration of God's dealings with us today. God allowed the testing time to come into the life of this man in order to bring him to the point of uncompromising faith and devotion to His will. God often permits the testing time to come into our lives today for the same purpose. He desires to draw us close to Himself and wills that we be conformed to the image of His blessed Son. May we submit ourselves, as did Abraham, so that God may become all in all.

9 Genesis 22:1-14

~~~~~~

The Testing of Abraham

INTRODUCTION

STUDY GOAL

CONCLUSION

INTRODUCTION

An interesting story has been told concerning a certain blacksmith of days gone by who received Christ as his Saviour. Yet for some strange reason, following his conversion this man's life seemed to be filled with an endless string of troubles and trials of every description. One of his unbelieving neighbors noticed this and stopped by the shop one day to mock him. "Blacksmith," the neighbor said, "why is it that you have so much trouble? Since you've joined the church and changed your way of living, you've had twice as many troubles as before. I thought you said that it paid to serve the Lord. I thought that when a man gave his life to God, his troubles were over. Yet you have more than ever. Why do you have so much trouble?"

This was not an easy question to answer, but the blacksmith had one ready. First he picked up a piece of steel that lay on the floor. And then he said, "My friend, do you see this piece of steel? I am going to use it for the springs of a carriage. But before it can be used, it has to be tempered with fire. And in order to do that I will have to put it into the furnace and heat it red hot. And then when I see that it will take temper, I will have to hammer it, and pound it, and twist it into shape until it becomes suitable for the carriage." At this point, the blacksmith paused, and then he made the following application: He said, "Now, neighbor, the same is true of me. God has saved me for a lot more than to have a good time in life. Oh, there is joy in the Christian life all right. But God has saved me so that I might serve Him. And in order that I might become a useful servant, just like this piece of steel, God has to put me into the furnace of affliction and testing. He has to heat me red hot. And then He has to hammer and pound me, and bend me into shape until I become a useful servant. Now, neighbor," said the blacksmith, "I don't enjoy the troubles. I don't enjoy the trials. But this is simply God's way of putting the 'temper' of Christ in me!"

The blacksmith, of course, gave a very wise answer, for through the years God has had only one way of putting the "temper" of Christ in us, and this is through the experience of testing and trial.

This thought will be graphically illustrated by the experience of Abraham as recorded in the passage that we will look at today. Someone has well said that Abraham is the man in the Bible whom God tested as no other. This statement is not merely a commentator's exaggeration. Instead, God did test Abraham in a most severe way. In our earlier lessons we learned that there were three specific promises that were a part of the Abrahamic covenant. First, there was the promise of the *land* of Canaan. All the land of Canaan extending from the River of Egypt to the Euphrates was one day to belong to Abraham. Secondly, there was a promise of a *blessing.* Abraham's life was to become a blessing to the whole world. And finally contained in the covenant was the promise of a *seed.* Abraham was to have a son, and that son in turn was to bless the whole world.

Now, concerning each of these three promises, God tested Abraham severely. In the case of the land, for example, God had no more than given His promise than we read in Genesis 12 that there was a famine in the land and that Abraham had to go down to Egypt to find food. In the case of the blessing, God had no more than given His promise than we read that there was "strife between the herdmen of Abram's cattle and the herdmen of Lot's cattle" (Gen. 13:7). At this point, it appeared that Abraham's life would turn out to be anything but a blessing. The same was true of the third of God's promises, the promise of the seed. God tested His man on this point over and over again in order to force him to walk by faith and not by sight.

In the section before us, God is now about to present Abraham with the most severe test of his life to see whether he would walk by faith.

STUDY GOAL

The purpose of our study is to examine the testings of Abraham in an attempt to determine God's purposes for testings in our lives today. The story of this chapter is a familiar one, but the student of the Word should not allow the familiarity of the material to distract from this important spiritual lesson.

I. The Testing of Faith (Gen. 22:1-2)

"And it came to pass after these things, that God did tempt Abraham, and said unto him, Abraham: and he said, Behold, here I am" (Gen. 22:1).

Our attention is captured immediately by the opening words of this verse where we are told that "after these things . . . God did *tempt* Abraham." On the surface, this statement may be somewhat disturbing to the casual reader because of the statement of James 1:13 where the Bible says, "Let no man say when he is tempted, I am tempted of God; for God cannot be tempted with evil, *neither tempteth he any man.*" How can these two statements be reconciled? Genesis 22:1 says that God "tempted" Abraham, yet the New Testament teaches that God never "tempts" any man.

The answer to the problem is a proper understanding of the use of the word "tempt" as it appears in the Bible. This word is used in two entirely different senses in the Word of God. In some instances the word is used in an evil sense meaning an enticement to sin or a solicitation to that which is evil. God, of course, never "tempts" men in this sense. He never entices men to do that which is contrary to the Word of God. The word "tempt," however, is used in a second way in the Bible. In other cases it is used in a good sense meaning "to test," or "to try," or "to prove" in order to determine the inner character of a person or thing. This latter usage is obviously the intention of the Holy Spirit in our text. God was not tempting Abraham in the sense that He was encouraging him to do that which was wrong or sinful. God does not do this. Only Satan tempts men in this way. But God was putting Abraham to the test; He was trying, or proving, him to see whether his faith was real and genuine.

This testing of Abraham's faith was a severe thing. In verse 2 the demands of God are clearly outlined in the words, "And he said, Take now thy son, thine only son Isaac, whom thou lovest, and get thee into the land Moriah; and offer him there for a burnt-offering upon one of the mountains which I will tell thee of." It is rather interesting to note the way in which God's demands are spelled out and the way in which God almost piles words on top of words in order to make His will crystal clear. It is as though God were saying (to paraphrase), "Abraham . . . take now thy son, thine only son. Yes, Abraham, I mean Isaac . . . that son for whom you prayed, and waited, and trusted . . . that son whom you love. Take him and get to Mount Moriah, and there offer him for a burnt offering unto me." It appears that God wanted His demands to be crystal clear. There was to be no mistake. And so, in unmistakable terms, God's demands are spelled out.

One could well wonder what Abraham's *immediate* reaction was to such a command. The Bible does not give the answer to this question, but without a doubt these words must have stabbed like a knife into the heart of Abraham. For years he had prayed and waited on God for this boy. In our earlier studies, we learned that God's original promise came when Abraham was 75 years of age. But instead of keeping His promise immediately, God made Abraham wait for over 25 years before fulfilling this promise. And during those 25 years, Abraham must have prayed, and waited, and trusted God. And then, finally after 25 years of waiting, God kept His promise and Isaac was born. What rejoicing there must have been in the house of Abraham! God had finally kept His promise and had given a son. No doubt during the years that Isaac grew to manhood, he became his father's pride and joy. In every sense of the word, Isaac was the most prized possession that Abraham had. And yet in the face of all this, God now was laying His hand on the most precious thing in Abraham's life, and He was saying, "Abraham, if you really love Me, give Me back that boy. Get to Mount Moriah and offer him there as a burnt offering unto me!" What staggering words these must have been to this man of faith!

In considering the experience of Abraham, it is important that we see here something of a pattern which God often follows in His dealings with His children. In the case of Abraham, God laid His hand on the most precious possession in his life, and He said, "Abraham, if you love me, give me that!" The Lord often deals with us in the same way. When He desires to speak to us, He often lays His hand on the thing that is dearest to us or the most precious possession we own, and He will say to us, "Believer, if you really love Me, then let Me have this precious possession!" In so doing, the Lord's intention is not to be harsh with us. Instead, this is His way of bringing us to the place where we put Him first in everything.

II. The Effect of Faith (Gen. 22:3-5)

The effect of Abraham's faith is obvious just from a simple reading of these three verses. In the case of Abraham, the effect of faith was simple and explicit obedience. Verse 3 indicates that Abraham rose up "early in the morning" (and the implication is that it was the morning after the command of God was given); he made the proper preparations and in obedience started out for Mount Moriah. And nowhere in the entire account is there a breath of complaint, or bitterness, or protest on Abraham's part. Instead, he simply rose up and followed the directions of the Lord without a word. Some commentators even insist that Abraham may not have told Sarah where he was going. Instead, in explicit obedience he took his boy in hand and started for Mount Moriah.

It is often asked, "But how could Abraham do such a thing? Didn't he love this boy? If so, then how could he bring himself to do such a thing?" Some have answered by saying that Abraham believed that once they got to the top of

Mount Moriah, God would provide an animal or substitute of another kind. This is doubtful. Abraham did not know about the ram caught in the thicket until later on in the story. Others have tried to answer this question by saying that Abraham believed that when they got to the top of Mount Moriah, God would somehow intervene and Isaac would not need to be slain. This is doubtful, too. Instead, the implication of these verses seems to be that Abraham left home that morning fully expecting that the moment would come when he would have to take his boy in hand, tie him to an altar, and plunge a dagger into his heart. But how could Abraham do such a thing? The answer to this question is given in Hebrews 11:17-19: "By faith Abraham, when he was tried, offered up Isaac: and he that had received the promises offered up his only begotten son. Of whom it was said, That in Isaac shall thy seed be called: *accounting that God was able to raise him up, even from the dead*; from whence also he received him in a figure."

The language of these words is unmistakable. The answer to our question is that by faith Abraham believed God would miraculously raise Isaac from the dead after he had killed him! This is truly an amazing thing, for God had not given Abraham one iota of assurance that Isaac would ever come back from Mount Moriah alive. And yet somehow this man of God simply clung to the Lord that day, and in his heart he was saying, "I don't understand all of this. I don't understand why God has asked me to give up my boy. But I do know that He promised to make of me a great nation, and I believe Him. And so whether this makes sense or not, I will obey. And I believe that God will keep His promise by raising him back from the dead!"

One certainly cannot help but admire the simple faith of this man of God, particularly in the light of the day in which he lived. Let us remember that this man had no written Bible to turn to as we have today. The Word of God had not as yet been written. Further, he didn't enjoy many of the spiritual privileges that we enjoy today. Instead, all that Abraham had to go by was the bare promise of God given some 50 or perhaps even 60 years before. But this was enough, and so in faith he stepped out, trusting that God would keep His Word! May the Lord enable us to walk with Him in the same kind of explicit obedience!

III. The Conflict of Faith (Gen. 22:6-10)

One cannot read these verses without somehow feeling that he has walked on holy ground. These words, in many respects, are some of the most moving verses that can be found anywhere in the Bible. According to verse 6, in time, Abraham and Isaac, along with the servants who accompanied them, arrived at the place appointed by God. So, after speaking to the young men, Abraham laid the wood on Isaac's shoulders, and they started up the mountainside together. In time, according to verse 7, Isaac asked the question Abraham was afraid that he would ask. He said, "Father . . . Behold the fire and the wood: but where is the lamb for a burnt-offering?" These words, without question must have burned like a fire in the heart of Abraham. But he gave an answer. He said, "My son, God will provide himself a lamb for a burnt-offering."

These words have been explained in various ways by Bible commentators. Some men feel that Abraham was still hoping against hope that God would provide a lamb or some other kind of animal instead of Isaac. This is doubtful. Instead, Abraham had completely resigned himself to the fact that the moment would come when he would have to kill his son in obedience to God. Hebrews 11:17 says that "by faith Abraham . . . *offered up Isaac.*" In the mind of Abraham, Isaac was as good as dead. He had completely resigned himself to the fact that Isaac would die. Other students of the Bible believe that Abraham was looking forward to the day when God would provide His Son, the Lord Jesus Christ, for the sins of the world. This is a possibility. However, it appears to this author that so far as Abraham was concerned that day, there would be no other sacrifice except Isaac. As indicated, Abraham sincerely believed that the moment would come when he would have to prepare the altar, tie his son to it, and then plunge a dagger into his son's heart in obedience to God.

One can well wonder what kind of thoughts must have passed through the mind of Abraham as he saw Isaac on the altar and as he stood there with the dagger in his hand. Certainly if there was ever a conflict of emotions in the heart of a man, it must have been so in the case of Abraham. To be sure, he did have the promise of God. But this was his only son—a son for whom he had prayed, and hoped, and trusted. And now everything seemed to be lost. Without question, thoughts like this must have passed through the mind of Abraham that day. And yet in the end, faith was victorious. Abraham took the knife and he prepared to obey God with it.

Needless to say, God always has a reward for this kind of faith and explicit obedience. And we read of Abraham's reward in verses 11 to 14.

IV. The Reward of Faith (Gen. 22:11-14)

These verses need little or no comment except for the reading of them. They are easily understood just by a simple reading of the text. God had put Abraham to one of the most severe tests that any man ever endured by asking him to part with the most precious thing in life to him. In faith, Abraham obeyed this command of God to the very letter. And now God rewarded him by sparing Isaac; and a ram caught in the thicket was offered up instead.

CONCLUSION

Many personal applications of the truths of this chapter may be applied to our hearts. Three in particular, however, are to be noted.

To begin with, the experience of Abraham on Mount Moriah is a beautiful illustration of another event that took place nearly 2,000 years later outside the walls of Jerusalem, where God the Father offered His beloved Son, the Lord Jesus

Christ, as a sin offering. In this respect, Abraham is a perfect type of God the Father. For just as he was willing to part with the most precious thing in life to him, God the Father willingly gave the most precious Gift that has ever been given to men; namely, the Lord Jesus Christ. Isaac in turn is a perfect type of Christ the Saviour. For just as Isaac willingly submitted to Abraham without murmur or complaint, so the Lord Jesus Christ willingly gave His life for our sin. Finally, even Mount Moriah is a perfect type of Calvary where Christ died. Many Bible students believe that Mount Calvary where Christ died was located somewhere on the slopes of Mount Moriah. So just as Abraham and Isaac walked up Mount Moriah on this particular day in order that Isaac might die, so many years later another Man walked up the slopes of Mount Calvary to die. And that Man was none other than Christ Himself, God's most precious gift to men. Thanks be to God for His unspeakable Gift given without reservation!

A second application of this chapter can be made. Just as Abraham did not count any sacrifice too great to make in order to prove his devotion, so our surrender and dedication ought to be full and complete. This is a simple truth, yet many of us limit our yielding to the Lord. We say, "I'll go where you want me to go, dear Lord," or "I'll be what you want me to be," and at the same time are ready to veto the will of God should He call upon us to go where we don't want to go and be what we don't want to be. Such "dedication" is not real dedication, and it only becomes real when we are willing to surrender to the will of God as did Abraham.

Someone has well pointed out that there was nothing wrong with Abraham's love for Isaac. And in like manner there may be nothing inherently wrong with the "Isaacs" to which *we* cling—loved ones, ambition, position, wealth, pleasure, and so on. There is nothing intrinsically wrong with any of these things. And yet when they interfere with God's will for our lives, we must lay them aside and submit to the Lord without reservation. What "Isaac" are you clinging to, my friend?

Perhaps only you and God know the answer to this question. Whatever that "Isaac" may be, may God give you grace to let it go and to submit fully to His blessed will.

This symbolic chapter has yet a third application that can be made. As indicated earlier, sometimes in order to put the "temper" of Christ in us, God has to place us in the furnace of affliction and testing. This certainly was so in the life of Abraham. God practically broke this man completely by laying His hand on the most precious thing in his life. And yet all of this was simply a part of God's plan to mold and shape Abraham into a useful servant. Perhaps, dear reader, you find yourself in similar circumstances. Perhaps God has laid His hand on the dearest thing in life to you. If so, as did Abraham, submit to the testing that God has sent, learn the lesson that He has in mind, and then walk in loving obedience to His will.

> "Oh, the bitter pain and sorrow
> That a time could ever be,
> When my proud heart said to Jesus,
> All of self and none of Thee.

> "But He found me, I beheld Him
> Hanging on the accursed tree,
> And my trembling heart then whispered
> Some for self and some for Thee.

> "But day by day, His tender mercy
> Wooing, loving, full and free,
> Drew me closer, closer 'til I whispered
> Less of self and more of Thee.

> "Higher than the highest mountain
> Deeper than the deepest sea,
> Lord at last thy love has conquered
> Now it's none of self, and all of Thee."

10 Genesis 24

A Bride for Isaac

INTRODUCTION

STUDY GOAL

    I.   **Abraham's Instructions (Gen. 24:1-9)**
        A.   A strict prohibition (24:1-4).
        B.   A confident faith (24:5-9).

    II.   **Eliezer's Obedience (Gen. 24:10-49)**
        A.   His zealous interest (24:10-14).
        B.   His gracious manner (24:15-33).
        C.   His loving faithfulness (24:34-49).
        D.   His blessed antitype.

   III.   **Rebekah's Consent (Gen. 24:50-60)**

   IV.   **Isaac's Joy (Gen. 24:61-67)**

CONCLUSION

INTRODUCTION

In the section before us, we will look briefly into the life of the second of four outstanding characters found in the Book of Genesis. As indicated earlier in our studies, in the second major division of the book, chapters 12 to 50, there are *four outstanding characters:* Abraham, Isaac, Jacob, and Joseph. Having already considered the life of Abraham, we turn now to the second of these four outstanding men; namely, to Isaac, the son of Abraham.

Isaac, in comparison to the other three outstanding characters of this section of the Book of Genesis, is a rather plain and ordinary man. His father, Abraham, was a very strong, dominating personality. And in like manner, Isaac's son Jacob was also a very strong leader and commander of men. In contrast, however, Isaac was just an "average" man. Someone has well said that a great man's son is seldom great; and when both father and son are men of great importance, they are conspicuous exceptions to the general rule. This general rule certainly was true of Isaac. He was the ordinary son of an extraordinary father, and he was the ordinary father of an extraordinary son. But he himself was just a plain average man. The life of Isaac ought to serve as an encouragement to those who tend to be discouraged because of the lack of great personal qualities. Many feel that because they lack unusual intelligence, or unusual cleverness, or an unusual personality, that it is therefore impossible or unusual for them to accomplish anything worthwhile in life. Such, of course, is not the case. God can use even "common" folks to accomplish His will (see Zech. 4:6).

In studying the life of Isaac, attention will be given only to the story of his marriage to Rebekah as recorded in Genesis 24. This account serves as a convenient dividing line in Isaac's life. The story of Isaac's life begins in Genesis 21 and ends in Genesis 35. However, much of the story of his early life is intermingled with that of his father, Abraham. And much of his later life merges into that of his children. The story of his marriage to Rebekah, however, seems to be a convenient dividing point in the record and, therefore, we will concentrate our efforts on this aspect of his life.

STUDY GOAL

The purpose of our study for today is to examine carefully the beautiful story of how Abraham found a bride for his son, and to learn from it the ways in which God leads His children even today. Attention will also be given to some of the typical aspects of the chapter.

I. Abraham's Instructions (Gen. 24:1-9)

In order to fully appreciate these verses, it is necessary for us to completely forget marriage customs as they are known in our land today. Today a young man will seek out the bride of his choice and then will attempt to woo and win her for himself. In Abraham's day, the parents normally arranged for the marriages of their children. It would have been an unusual thing indeed for Abraham to have allowed Isaac to select his own bride. This custom then explains the procedure of this chapter. Isaac was now 40 years of age (see Gen. 25:20) and still single. Abraham, in contrast, was an old man approaching the evening of life. And the time had now come for him to arrange for the marriage of his son.

In considering the arrangements which Abraham made, two items in particular are to be noted concerning his instructions.

A. A strict prohibition (24:1-4). "And Abraham said unto his eldest servant of his house . . . I will make thee swear by the Lord, the God of heaven, and the God of the earth, that thou shalt not take a wife unto my son of the daughters of the Canaanites, among whom I dwell: but thou shalt go into my country, and to my kindred, and take a wife unto my son Isaac" (Gen. 24:2-4).

It should be said to Abraham's credit that the one thing he wanted to avoid above all costs was a marriage between his son and a Canaanite woman. The Canaanites belonged to that branch of Noah's family upon whom the curse of God resided (see Gen. 9:25). Therefore, under no circumstances whatsoever was Isaac to marry a woman of this line. Instead, the servant is instructed to return to the land of Mesopotamia, from where Abraham had originally come, and there he was to find a bride for Isaac. The objection is sometimes raised that Abraham's relatives back in Mesopotamia were hardly better than the Canaanites of the land, for the kinsmen of Abraham were idolaters (see Josh. 24:2; Gen. 31:30-34). While this may have been true, at least Abraham's relatives in Mesopotamia were not under the curse of God. Instead they were the descendants of Shem, through whom God had promised to work (see Gen. 9:26). A bride for Isaac was, therefore, to come from among these people.

Abraham's strict refusal to allow his son Isaac to enter into a "mixed" marriage with a daughter of the land is a good illustration of the kind of caution that parents and young people need today. In many cases, for example, parents do not warn their children early enough and strongly enough against a marriage with one of another faith or with one of no faith at all. In addition, Christian young people who marry often give little or no thought to the spiritual life of their partner, and will even enter into a marriage contract with one who is a professed unbeliever. Experience has shown that such a relationship will inevitably result in heartache and grief to the saved partner. How much better to think and plan, and choose carefully and prayerfully before entering into such a life commitment.

In this connection, also, perhaps some of our Protestant churches have something to learn from the Roman Catholic Church. The Roman Catholic Church is much more strict than most Protestant churches in the matter of the marriages of its young people. It believes that its faith is the only saving faith. And therefore the marriage of its young people must always be on its terms. The Roman church, of course, is wrong in its thinking on this point, but they are right in their insistence that young people must think and choose seriously and wisely when seeking a life partner. Perhaps many of our Protestant churches have been too "flabby" in their convictions on this point and need to make their demands a great deal more emphatic.

B. A confident faith (24:5-9). A second item to be noticed in this section is the confident faith of Abraham. In verse 5, the servant suggests a possible problem that might arise in his search for a bride for Isaac. Suppose that the chosen bride does not agree to leave her home in Mesopotamia to start a new life in Canaan. What was he to do then? It is to this question that Abraham gives his confident answer of faith.

"And Abraham said unto him, Beware thou that thou bring not my son thither again. *The Lord God of heaven,* which took me from my father's house, and from the land of my kindred, and which spake unto me, and that sware unto me, saying, Unto thy seed will I give this land; *he shall send his angel before thee, and thou shalt take a wife unto my son from thence*" (Gen. 24:6-7).

In these words, Abraham confidently looked to God Himself, the Source of all power and grace, to bring the servant's mission to a successful conclusion. Abraham's faith, however, was not a blind one. Instead, there were two things which led him to depend on God. First, there were the blessings and the provisions of the past. It was God who had called Abraham from his father's house and from the land of his kindred years before. It was God who had provided for Abraham's every need through the years. Since this was true, what God had done in the past, He could certainly do again. Second, Abraham was led to rely upon God because of His promise for the future. Years before, on the occasion of the sacrifice of Isaac, God had promised the land of Canaan to Abraham's seed and had sealed it with an oath (see Gen. 22:15-18). Abraham doubtless remembered this promise as well. So, by recalling God's past blessings and by the encouragement of God's promises, Abraham voiced his deep faith in quiet confidence. The servant would not need to return without a bride of God's choice. Nor would Isaac need to leave the land of Canaan to claim his bride. Instead, Abraham believed in his heart that God was going to answer.

Abraham's faith, as recorded in this section, is certainly beautiful to behold. Recall that he did not have the written Word of God as we have today. Nor did he enjoy many of the spiritual privileges that we enjoy today. Instead, all that he had was the bare promise of God-given years before, plus the encouragement of God's leading in his life. But this was enough. So in quiet confidence he declared his faith. What an assurance this ought to be to us today to "step out" in faith in times of need, relying completely upon the Lord.

II. Eliezer's Obedience (Gen. 24:10-49)

The servant of this chapter is not named. However, there is a good possibility that it was Eliezer, last mentioned in Genesis 15:2 where he is seen as the manager of Abraham's household. If so, then Eliezer held a long and enviable record of service with Abraham. In fact, he may have served him for as long as 80 consecutive years, an enviable record indeed! Several specific items are worthy of mention concerning the servant and his work.

A. His zealous interest (24:10-14). It is interesting to observe from these verses that Eliezer had completely identified himself with the plan and the purpose of his master, Abraham. Here was a man who was zealously involved in the work of his master, and one who delighted to do his bidding. Eliezer's obedience was not a slavish kind of service. Instead, it is evident that he found real joy in serving Abraham. This is seen in several instances in the text. To begin with, Eliezer's zeal is seen in the promptness with which he set out upon his errand (v. 10). His zeal is also seen in his earnest prayer for guidance (vv. 12-14). The prayer of these verses is one of the most beautiful prayers of Scripture, and the zeal of the servant is seen especially because of the emphasis on his master in the prayer and a desire that God would show kindness to Abraham.

The zeal of Eliezer is a pattern or a model for all who are called upon to work for the Lord. Our zeal and interest in the Lord's work ought to be equal if not greater than that of the servant of Abraham. Our service for Christ ought not to be performed in a slavish manner. Nor should it be offered grudgingly or reluctantly. Instead, it ought to be a delight to do the will of our Lord and Master, Jesus Christ (see Ps. 40:7-8).

B. His gracious manner (24:15-33). One cannot help but see here the gracious manner of the servant. Note for example, his courtesy and gentlemanly behavior in verse 17. The manner in which we conduct our Christian service, with or without courtesy, has a great deal to do with its success or failure. Our cause and our message may be good, but if it is not presented with courtesy and consideration, it will accomplish very little. Note further, the patience of the servant as illustrated in verse 21. Doubtless one of the reasons our service for Christ is so often unfruitful is that we are in a hurry too much of the time, and because we force matters ahead of God's time. Still further, note the reverence and the thankfulness of the servant as seen in verses 26 and 27, when he realized that his prayer had been answered and that he had been guided by the Lord every step of the way. Without question, one of the reasons so few of our prayers are answered is that the Lord cannot trust us with the answer. Instead of returning thanks and giving Him the glory when the answer is given, so often we selfishly steal the glory that rightfully belongs to the Lord. Finally, note the intense earnestness of this servant as seen in verse 33. Here was one who could not so much as eat or rest until he had declared the purpose of his mission. His master's cause and work came first.

Once again, the gracious manner of this servant ought to serve as a very excellent pattern or model for us to follow in our service for Christ. How much more fruitful our service would be if we were to develop these basic qualities.

C. His loving faithfulness (24:34-49). The general overall impression that is created by these verses is that the servant Eliezer was one who was completely faithful to his master and to his task. To begin with, he stated who he was (v. 34). Secondly, he was loud and enthusiastic in his praise of his master (vv. 35-36). And finally, he faithfully declared the purpose of his mission and offered a definite choice to the loved ones of Rebekah—whom he had met at the well.

The faithfulness of Eliezer to his master and to his work is the kind of goal for which we should strive in our service for Christ. The Lord may not use us to reach the masses of earth with the message of the Gospel. Instead, His plan for us may involve a seemingly unimportant and obscure place in the harvest field. Regardless of where the Lord puts us, however, our purpose should be to be faithful to the message and to the calling that is ours from Him (see I Cor. 4:2).

D. His blessed antitype. Many students of the Bible see in the servant Eliezer a beautiful type of the person and work of the Holy Spirit, the third person of the Godhead. While caution needs to be exercised so that not all Scripture is "spiritualized," there are some very striking comparisons that can be made. Dr. M. R. DeHaan, in his book *Adventures in Faith, Studies in the Life of Abraham,* has made quite an exhaustive study of this subject. While it is not our intention to pursue this kind of study at length, the following are some of the comparisons which may be briefly presented:

1. The name "Eliezer" means "God's helper." This is likewise the ministry of the Holy Spirit today. It is His work to bring God's chosen ones to Christ (see John 16:7-11).

2. Eliezer was sent by Abraham, the father, in behalf of his son Isaac. The Holy Spirit, in like manner, has been sent by the Father in behalf of the Son (see John 14:16-17, 26).

3. Eliezer was given full and complete authority to administer the affairs of Isaac and to seek out a bride for him. So, too, the Holy Spirit possesses the full authority of deity. He

is God of very gods and equal with the Father and the Son.

4. There was perfect agreement and understanding between Abraham, the father, and Eliezer, the servant. So it is with the Holy Spirit today. There is perfect agreement and understanding between Him and the other members of the Trinity (see John 16:13).

5. Eliezer was a praying servant. So the Spirit of God helps us in the ministry of prayer (see Rom. 8:26).

III. Rebekah's Consent (Gen. 24:50-60)

According to the customs of the day, the father and the brother of the bride-to-be had the right to make the final decisions in the arranging of the marriage contract. For this reason, the servant approached them first to secure their consent in verses 50 to 54. However, when Eliezer declared his desire to be sent on his way with Rebekah immediately and without delay, this was another matter entirely. And as a result, Rebekah's family wisely decided to put this matter up to her (v. 57). Rebekah's response was immediate and without hesitation. She announced that she was ready to leave with Abraham's servant (v. 58). So she is sent away with the servant with the blessing of the family.

In reading these verses, one cannot help but admire the simple courage of Rebekah in this decision. Note, for example, the following three facts which stand out in the narrative: She was asked to go with a person whom she had never met before. She was asked to marry a man whom she had never met. She was asked to leave her home and to go to a country which she had never seen before and from which she would never return. Yet despite these three conditions she said, "I will go," and this settled the matter. Her faith was simple, absolute, and final. The faith and dedication of Rebekah in this instance certainly is the kind of trusting faith which the Lord desires to see in us. May our faith in Him be just as simple and resolute as that of Rebekah.

IV. Isaac's Joy (Gen. 24:61-67)

In reading through the narrative of this chapter, one begins to wonder about the feelings and desires of Isaac during this period of time when the servant is away seeking the bride. How does he feel, and what preparations is he making for the coming of the bride? This question is answered in part in the words of verse 63, where we are told that "Isaac went out to meditate in the field at the eventide." Some students suggest that the word "meditate" means "to pray." If so, then doubtless this means that Isaac had spent these days during the absence of the servant in prayer to God, asking for the success of the servant's mission. This prayer was answered by God in completeness, for verse 67 says, "Isaac brought her into his mother Sarah's tent, and took Rebekah, and she became his wife; and he loved her: and Isaac was comforted after his mother's death." What joy and rejoicing must have .been present in this household! It is apparent that God had led each step of the way and that the bride of His choice had been provided.

CONCLUSION

Many conservative Bible scholars see in this chapter a beautiful illustration of the work of God the Father in selecting a Bride (the Church) for His Son, the Lord Jesus Christ. While caution must be exercised so that not all Scripture is "spiritualized," there are some very striking comparisons that can be made here. Note, for example, the following: (1) In the chapter can be seen the purpose of the father. Abraham had but one primary purpose; namely, to seek a bride for his son. In like manner, God the Father has the same purpose in mind for His Son (see Matt. 22:2). (2) In the chapter can be seen the position of the son. The son is the father's one and only thought. So it is with the Son of God (see Eph. 1:20-22). (3) In the chapter can be seen the prospects of the bride. The bride was thought of even before she knew it (see Eph. 1:4 for the application). (4) In the chapter can be seen the proclamation of the servant. The servant had but one primary task; namely, to seek out the bride. The Holy Spirit performs this work today (see John 16:13-14). (5) In the chapter can be seen the power of the message (see John 12:32 for the application). (6) In the chapter can be seen the prospect of a new home for the bride. The Bride of Christ in like manner looks forward with joy to the new home of heaven. Dr. Scofield's note in the *Scofield Reference Bible* supplies an abundance of material on this point.

This chapter is also a blessed illustration of the way in which God desires to direct our lives. Whether it be the choice of a life partner, or a life work, or a place to live, God is personally interested and concerned. What a blessed thought this is! This truth is graphically illustrated in the experience of Abraham's servant. Humanly speaking, the chances that Eliezer would find a bride for Isaac as he did were practically nil. Yet he found her as God directed in his life. The Lord can lead and direct in our lives in the same manner if we are willing to let Him. If this be true, then may we so place ourselves at His disposal so that He can lead and direct us as He so much desires to do.

11 Genesis 25–35

Jacob, the Man Beloved of God

INTRODUCTION

STUDY GOAL

I. **The Men in Jacob's Life**
    A. Isaac.
    B. Esau.
    C. Laban.

II. **The Women in Jacob's Life**
    A. Rebekah.
    B. Rachel.

III. **The God in Jacob's Life**
    A. Bethel (28:10-15).
    B. Jabbok (32:22-32).
    C. Bethel (35:1-5).
    D. Beersheba (46:1-4).

CONCLUSION

INTRODUCTION

The story of the life of Jacob, the beloved of God, can scarcely be overemphasized. His importance is clearly seen by the fact that the record of his life is woven into some 26 chapters of the Book of Genesis, chapters 25 to 50. It is true that the record of his early life is intermingled with that of his father Isaac. And the record of his later life merges into that of his son Joseph. But the story of Jacob's life is interwoven into at least this much of the Book of Genesis. This becomes a rather significant point when a comparison is made with the much shorter portions devoted to the life stories of both Abraham and Isaac. The story of Abraham's life, by comparison, is told in some 15 chapters, and only some 5 or 6 chapters are devoted to Isaac. In contrast, the Holy Spirit used some 26 chapters to tell the story of Jacob's life. This is as long as most of the New Testament Gospels. In addition, it has been said that the name "Jacob" appears more frequently than the name of any other man in the Bible with the exception of the names of God. These facts would certainly indicate something of the importance of this man's life.

In our handling of Jacob's life, an attempt will be made to present a general survey of his life. No attempt will be made to handle any one passage in detail. Rather, like an artist with his brush, the material will be presented in great sweeping strokes so as to provide a general outline of the life Jacob lived.

STUDY GOAL

We suggest that the story of Jacob's life may be presented as something of a drama in three acts. The first act has to do with the men in Jacob's life—men whom he knew and loved or despised. Act two of the story of Jacob has to do with the women in his life—women who influenced him, either for good or for evil. Finally, act three will have to do with the God in Jacob's life, and will deal with the various spiritual experiences which he had—experiences which made him the man that he was. The aim in our study is to survey the life of Jacob in order to determine why he became the man of importance that he became.

I. The Men in Jacob's Life

Doubtless there were many men who influenced Jacob in various ways. The lives of three men in particular are to be noted in our study.

A. Isaac. The first man of importance in Jacob's life was his father, Isaac. In our earlier studies, we attempted to show that Isaac, in many respects, was a rather "colorless" individual. He was a rather plain, ordinary man who lacked the strength of character and personality of his father Abraham and of his son Jacob. Isaac's father Abraham, of course, was a very strong, dominating personality. And in like manner, Isaac's son Jacob was a very strong leader and commander of men. But in contrast, Isaac was a rather quiet, passive man whose life served as something of a "buffer" between the life of Abraham and the life of Jacob.

Hebrews 11:20 speaks of Isaac as a man of faith. And there were times when Isaac gave real evidence of a deep abiding faith in God. Genesis 24:63 and Genesis 26:17-25 are good illustrations of his faith. However, there were many other times when Isaac was definitely unspiritual in his attitude and outlook. An outstanding example of one of these times is the story of the stolen blessing recorded in Genesis 27. Under normal conditions, in our handling of this story, we are inclined to place all of the blame for the stolen blessing upon Jacob and his scheming mother Rebekah. Without question, Jacob and his mother Rebekah should share a part of the blame for this act of deception. But a part of the blame should also be placed upon the shoulders of Isaac because of his unspiritual attitude. Earlier in Genesis 25:21-23, on the occasion of the birth of Jacob and Esau, God had said to Rebekah, "Two nations are in thy womb, and two manner of people shall be separated from thy bowels; and the one people shall be stronger than the other people; and *the elder shall serve the younger.*" The language of these words is unmistakable. Jacob was definitely God's choice. Yet apparently when the time came for the patriarchal blessing to be passed on, Isaac conveniently "forgot" about God's instructions, and he determined to give the blessing to his favorite son, Esau, instead.

Various attempts have been made to defend Isaac for this action. Some have suggested that Rebekah had never informed Isaac of the instructions of the Lord in Genesis 25:23, and therefore he was unaware that the "elder was to serve the younger." Others have suggested that perhaps Isaac had misunderstood the message of the Lord. Still others have suggested that perhaps in his old age Isaac had become a bit senile and was experiencing lapses in memory, and therefore, he had forgotten about God's words. These attempts to defend Isaac seem rather empty and fruitless. Instead, the best explanation is that at this point in his life, Isaac had become spiritually weak and unspiritual in his vision. He had a natural affection for his eldest son, Esau, that he would not deny. Isaac doubtless saw in Esau the kind of man that he had always wanted to be. Esau was a dashing, spirited, adventurous type of man. This is the kind of man Isaac had always wanted to be and yet had never become. So in spite of God's clear choice of Jacob, Isaac, filled with a heart of self-will, determined to frustrate God's plan by clinging to Esau, his favorite son. God, of course, overruled Isaac's desire, and doubtlessly later Isaac realized that he had been wrong and so resolutely refused to change his blessing once it had been given (see Gen. 27:33, 37; Heb. 12:17).

The influence of Isaac upon Jacob was nothing short of tremendous. Isaac made the same mistake that parents sometimes make today. He was an overfond parent, guilty of showing favoritism toward one member of the family. This attitude sowed seeds of dissention and mistrust in the family which later on wrought grief, heartache, and havoc for many years to come. How careful parents need to be in their attitudes toward each child in the home so as not to deprive any of the love and affection which is needed.

B. Esau. A second important man in Jacob's life was Esau. Esau has sometimes been portrayed as an admirable type of person. He has sometimes been presented as a dashing, adventurous, spirited individual who was attractive, generous, and thoroughly in love with life. Writers have sometimes pictured him as a kind of "man's man," an example of the ideal way of life.

While it is true that Esau may have possessed certain traits that are admirable, it is rather unfortunate that he should be glamorized and presented as a hero or an ideal man. Instead, the truth of the matter is that Esau was an earthy, worldly man who had no sense of spiritual values whatsoever. This is illustrated by several incidents from his life. To begin with, Esau's attitude toward his birthright, in Genesis 25:27-34, is an excellent illustration of Esau's unspiritual sense of values. In recent years, it has been learned that the family birthright involved at least three items:

1. The son who possessed the birthright was entitled to a double portion of the inheritance.

2. The son possessing the birthright was given the right to serve as the family priest. It was his privilege to be the elder of the family and to make all decisions of a spiritual nature.

3. The holder of the birthright became heir to the family's religious heritage and was thought to be one from whose line the Saviour would one day come.

While the first of these three blessings—the one having to do with the double portion of the inheritance—may have been desired by Esau, he apparently did not want the "headache" that went with the last two items. He was a man who had no appreciation whatever for spiritual values. To be associated with the line from which the Saviour would come meant nothing to him. Instead, Esau was a man of the world who lived only for the things of time instead of the things of eternity. Since this was so, Esau foolishly sold his birthright to his scheming brother Jacob for a bowl of stew. In this respect, Esau is typical of multitudes who live only for that which will gratify the body, with little or no thought for the hereafter.

A further incident which illustrates Esau's unspiritual approach to life is the tragic story of his marriage to two Hittite women recorded in Genesis 26:34-35. Esau's marriage to these women was in direct conflict with the desires of his parents and is another convincing indication that he was a worldly man who cared little for spiritual matters.

C. Laban. A third important man in Jacob's life was his uncle, Laban. The story of Jacob's association with Laban is recorded in Genesis chapters 29 to 31. These several chapters contain the well-known stories of Laban's dealings with Jacob, Jacob's marriage to two of Laban's daughters, the years of Jacob's service to Laban, and so on.

The Scriptures present Laban as a hard taskmaster. He was a covetous, grasping, self-seeking man who was more than a match for even a shrewd schemer like Jacob. The Lord doubtless used Laban to teach Jacob a great many lessons. Something of the same is often true today. God will sometimes see fit to send a "Laban" into our lives. The Christian, for example, may be forced to work alongside one who is mean, contemptible, and unfair. Or he may be called upon to live next door to one who is selfish and unreasonable, and who will not hesitate to trample on the rights of others in order to secure a selfish end. Under adverse circumstances like these, the Christian will often find himself growing and maturing spiritually as never before. The influence of Laban in Jacob's life may have had this kind of effect. Laban may have been sent deliberately into the life of Jacob by God in order to bring him to the end of himself and face to face with his own spiritual needs.

There were many other men in Jacob's life who influenced him profoundly, but the influence of these three—Isaac, Esau, and Laban—must have been tremendous. Jacob, of course, became a schemer. He was that by nature. But the influence of these may have encouraged this natural tendency. Jacob may have thought he *had* to deceive in order to get along with his father, his brother, and his uncle, Laban. While Jacob is not to be excused for his many sins, it is easy to see why he did what he did in so many instances.

II. The Women in Jacob's Life

Secondly, let us think briefly about the women in Jacob's life. There were several women who profoundly affected Jacob's life. Only two, however, are to be mentioned in our study.

A. Rebekah. Rebekah has often been called one of the ablest women in the Old Testament. She was a woman of strong will and strong character. However, she, like her son Jacob, was a sly one. (Jacob may have gotten his craftiness honestly!) This is illustrated in the story of the stolen blessing in Genesis 27, already referred to here earlier (see especially Gen. 27:5-17). It is rather obvious from these verses that Rebekah was leaving nothing to chance and very little to the Lord in order to make sure that her favorite son, Jacob, got all that was coming to him. It is true, of course, that she had the promise of God "on her side." The "elder was to serve the younger." However, instead of waiting on God to fulfill His promise, she felt that she needed to "help God out" a bit. So, she determined that she would not stop at anything to bring Jacob to the fore even if it meant sacrificing her husband, her son Esau, and her own principles. The steps which Rebekah took in this story were definitely unspiritual, and she paid dearly for her sin. Jacob was forced to leave home because of the wrath of Esau, and Rebekah never saw her son again. By the time he returned, she had already died.

The influence of Rebekah upon Jacob must have been staggering. Rebekah, like some parents today, had almost made an idol out of her son, and the open show of favoritism and the vying for affections in this home must have profoundly affected both Esau and Jacob.

B. Rachel. A second important woman in Jacob's life was Rachel. While Rachel, like her mother-in-law Rebekah, was a rather resourceful individual full of all sorts of plans and projects, she apparently was one of the few "bright spots" in Jacob's life. She was a woman whom Jacob loved dearly. This is seen in such passages as Genesis 29:16-20; 33:1-2. Jacob's love for Rachel perhaps reveals a different side of Jacob's life that deserves to be seen. His relationship to her may indicate that even Jacob was capable of great tenderness, devotion, and love at times. This is indicated by the fact that he didn't use any of his craft and scheming methods in order to get her. Much of that which Jacob possessed in life he had gotten by his own craft, cleverness, and deceit. But not so in the case of Rachel. Instead, he apparently had fallen so deeply in love with her that he offered to work for seven years in exchange for her hand (Gen. 29:18, 20). And even after Laban had deceived him by giving him Leah instead, Jacob was willing to serve for another seven years in order to gain the bride of his choice (Gen. 29:30). Jacob's relationship to her may indicate a depth of devotion and a strength of character that even he was capable of on occasion.

There were other women in Jacob's life—women like Leah, Bilhah, and Zilpah. However, outside of Rachel, who brought Jacob great joy, his relationship to the women in his life brought Jacob little else but suffering and heartache. The home into which he was born, the home of Isaac and Rebekah, had been a home filled with favoritism, dissention, and deceit. And Jacob's own home, with his several wives and many children, was marred with jealousy and wrangling between members of his family. Even Jacob's relationship to his favorite wife Rachel may have been filled with grief and sorrow. Genesis 29:31 reveals that she was barren for many years. And when finally the Lord did grant her the privilege of bearing children, she died in childbirth (see Gen. 35:16-20). The women in Jacob's life in all probability brought him little joy or comfort. Instead, in most cases, they brought him only grief.

III. The God in Jacob's Life

Jacob's experience with God is a marvelous illustration of God's plan and purpose to bring every believer to the point of spiritual maturity. When God began with Jacob, He had very little to work with. Jacob was a self-willed, stubborn man who was convinced that he could "get by" in life by his own cleverness and sharp wits. By a long and painful process, however, the Lord reduced Jacob to the point of nothingness. And at long last, Jacob yielded to God's will for his life. Several steps in this process will be noted briefly. Careful study of Genesis 25 to 50 will reveal that God appeared some seven different times to Jacob (see Gen. 28:10-15; 31:3; 32:1-2; 32:22-32; 35:1-2; 35:9-15; 46:1-4). Only four of these appearances will be discussed in our study.

A. Bethel (28:10-15). The first appearance which God made to Jacob was at a place called Bethel, and took place on the occasion of his flight from home because of the wrath of Esau. At this time, God made something of a formal announcement to Jacob that he would be the heir to the promises that had been given earlier to Isaac and to Abraham. No doubt Jacob had often heard about the Lord in his father's home. However, this is the first recorded instance in which we are told that he had any kind of personal contact with God. Was Jacob "saved" here at Bethel? We dare not be too dogmatic on this point, but it is quite possible that Jacob committed his life to the Lord on this occasion. See Genesis 48:3, which may support this position.

B. Jabbok (32:22-32). Someone has well said, "A sinner can be transformed into a child of God in an instant of time, but it takes a lifetime to manufacture a 'saint.'" This certainly would be so of Jacob. While he may have made a life commitment at Bethel in Genesis 28, the life which he lived following that experience indicates that there was still much work to be done before he would become strong and mature in faith. However, here in Genesis 32, Jacob learned one of the most important lessons of his life. The story of Jacob's wrestling with the angel has often been interpreted as an illustration of prevailing prayer. This interpretation, however, is wide of the mark. Note carefully Genesis 32:24. In this verse, we are not told that Jacob wrestled with God in order to secure some blessing. Instead, it was God who wrestled with Jacob in order to gain some object from him. What object was that? It was Jacob's will. The wrestling of this chapter was God's way of reducing Jacob to a sense of his nothingness, His way of causing him to see what a poor, helpless creature he was, and His way of teaching him that he must forget his cleverness and deceit forever. This plan and purpose of God was fulfilled, for from this point on, Jacob's scheming nature seems to have changed. From this point on, he became a mellowed and submissive man to a great degree.

C. **Bethel (35:1-5).** A second appearance was made to Jacob at Bethel. Years before, God had appeared to him at Bethel (see Gen. 28:10-15). But now God called him back to Bethel again, where the promises were confirmed to him again. No doubt the reason this second appearance became necessary was that between the first Bethel experience and this second one, Jacob had gone out of the land of Palestine and had lived for a time outside of the land of promise. God's promises were associated with the land of Palestine. So, upon his return to the land, it became necessary to reconfirm the covenant.

D. **Beersheba (46:1-4).** The final appearance which God made to Jacob took place at Beersheba toward the close of Jacob's life. Word had come that his long-lost son, Joseph, was a ruler in Egypt and that he was inviting him to come to live there. Jacob doubtless hesitated at this, for he remembered that Egypt had proved to be a snare to his grandfather, Abraham. So, God appeared to him with a special word of assurance. He was not to fear Egypt. Instead, God would go with him and would prosper him.

CONCLUSION

The life of Jacob is a graphic illustration of the plan and purpose of God to make of every believer a strong and mature saint. In Jacob's life, we can see the hand of God at work. We can see Him breaking, molding, and shaping this man from a crafty, scheming supplanter to a strong and stalwart saint. Jacob's training required many years and some painful experiences. But eventually he became a man beloved of God.

The plan of God for Jacob is little different from that of His plan for our lives. He wants to conform us, like Jacob, to the "image of His Son" (see Rom. 8:29). God's work in us, however, as it was with Jacob, may require many years and many painful experiences before we become saintly in our conduct and walk. As it was with Jacob, God has little to begin with when He deals with us. Most of us are full of the self-life. The self-life is strong and resists to the bitter end. But it is God's plan to bring us to the end of ourselves so that we may in turn become strong and mature in faith. May we not be guilty of resisting this, His plan and purpose for us. Instead, may we yield ourselves to His perfect plan that this purpose may be fulfilled in us.

12 Genesis 37–50

~~~~~~

The Story of Joseph

INTRODUCTION

STUDY GOAL

I.   Joseph and His Father

II. Joseph and His Brethren

III. Joseph and His Rejection
     A.   Joseph was sent by his father (37:13).
     B.   Joseph was conspired against (37:18).
     C.   Joseph was sold for money (37:25-28).

IV. Joseph and His Humiliation
     A.   Joseph became a servant (39:1-2).
     B.   Joseph was sorely tempted (39:7-12).
     C.   Joseph suffered for the sins of another
          (39:20–40:23).

V.   Joseph and His Exaltation
     A.   Joseph was duly exalted (41:39-44).
     B.   Joseph took a Gentile bride (41:45).
     C.   Joseph was reconciled to his brethren.

CONCLUSION

INTRODUCTION

The story of Joseph brings the Book of Genesis to a very wonderful conclusion. He is the last of the four outstanding men whose life stories appear in the second main section of the book (chapters 12-50). The story of Joseph's life is one of the best-loved stories of the Bible, and the record of his life is filled with an abundance of spiritual lessons.

In our handling of Joseph's life, no attempt will be made to retell the story. The story is so well known that this hardly seems necessary. Instead, an attempt will be made to point out some of the typical lessons which his life teaches us. Someone has well said that in studying the historical records of the Old Testament, it must be remembered that underneath and behind many of these records there are some great spiritual truths and lessons. The Bible was not written entirely to record the history of certain men or incidents, or to teach us moral and ethical lessons alone. Instead, the stories of the Old Testament often prefigure persons, or things, or truths which are later revealed in greater detail. While some caution needs to be observed in this kind of study so as not to "spiritualize" all of Scripture, the New Testament does allow for this type of Bible study (see I Cor. 10:11; II Tim. 3:16-17).

If this be true, then what typical lessons does the life of Joseph teach us? Most conservative students of the Bible see in Joseph a perfect type of Christ. It is true, of course, that nowhere in the New Testament are we told that the life of Joseph is typical of the Lord Jesus Christ. However, it is almost impossible to read the story without seeing the striking resemblances between these two important persons.

STUDY GOAL

The aim of our study for today is to review the familiar story of Joseph and to point out the resemblances between his life and the person and work of Christ. In pursuing this kind of study, the life of Joseph will be considered from several different viewpoints.

I. Joseph and His Father

"Now Israel loved Joseph more than all his children" (Gen. 37:3).

The relationship of Joseph to his father Jacob can best be described in the words of the text. Joseph was the beloved son of his father. And how Jacob must have loved Joseph! Jacob's love for Joseph is evident from several details in the story. To begin with, in Genesis 37:3 we are told that as a token of his love and esteem, Jacob prepared for Joseph a "coat of many colors." This latter phrase ought to be more properly translated "a long garment with sleeves." A working man in Palestine normally wore a short-sleeved garment that was rather short so as not to impede his movement. Joseph, however, was given this long, flowing garment that may have reached nearly to his ankles. A robe of this kind, to the Hebrew mind, was a symbol of royalty and privilege. And the garment was no doubt given by Jacob to his son as a token of his great love. Jacob's love for Joseph is also evidenced by his grief when he believed that Joseph had been devoured by wild beasts (see Gen. 37:31-35). And a further evidence of Jacob's love for Joseph is seen in Genesis 45:25-28 where Jacob determined to make the long journey to Egypt when he learned that his favorite son was yet alive.

How typical all this is of the Lord Jesus Christ! Just as Joseph was preeminent in the love of his father Jacob, so Christ is the well-beloved Son of God the Father. That this is true is evidenced by the fact that at least twice during our Lord's earthly ministry, the Father publicly affirmed his love for the Son. On the occasion of His baptism, as Jesus was about to enter His public ministry, the heavens were opened and the voice of the Father was heard saying, *"This is my beloved Son* in whom I am well pleased" (Matt. 3:17). Once again on the Mount of Transfiguration, the voice of the Father was heard conveying this same message (see Matt. 17:5). That Christ is the well-beloved Son in whom the

Father delights is also seen in many other passages of Scripture. See such passages as John 3:35; 5:20; 10:17; and Colossians 1:13.

II. Joseph and His Brethren

The relationship of Joseph to his brethren may best be expressed by the word "hatred." In Genesis 37, three times within the space of five verses, reference is made to the hatred of Joseph's brethren. In Genesis 37:4, we read, "*They hated him,* and could not speak peaceably unto him." Again in Genesis 37:5 we are told, "*And they hated him* yet the more." Finally, once again in Genesis 37:8 we read, "*And they hated him* yet the more for his dreams and for his words." A careful study of these various verses will reveal that the brethren of Joseph had two special reasons for their hatred of him. First, they hated Joseph as a *person* because of Jacob's special love for him. And second, they hated him for his *words.* In other words, they hated him first for what he *was* and second for what he *said.*

How typical this is of the person and work of Christ. When we turn to the record of the Gospels in the New Testament, we discover that our Lord's brethren according to the flesh, the Jews, hated Him for exactly the same two reasons. To begin with, the Jews of Jesus' day hated Him because of His person—or because of who He was. Several good illustrations of this may be cited. For example, in John 5:18 we read, "Therefore the Jews sought the more to kill him, because he not only had broken the sabbath, but said also that God was his Father, making himself equal with God." The wrath of the Jews on this occasion obviously was being directed against the *person* of Christ. They hated Him because of who He was. Further Scripture passages which illustrate the same truth are John 6:41; 10:30-31. In each of these references, the hatred of the Jews is directed against the person of Christ. And then secondly, the Lord Jesus Christ, just like Joseph of old, was hated because of His *words* or because of what He said. In John 7:7 Jesus said, "The world cannot hate you:

but *me it hateth, because I testify of it,* that the works thereof are evil." Luke 4:16-29 (note especially verses 28 and 29) and John 8:40 may also be used as illustrations of the hatred of the Jews for the words of Christ.

In these two regards, human nature hasn't changed very much through the years. Just as both Joseph and Christ were hated and despised because of who they were and because of what they said, so unsaved men today reject Christ for precisely the same two reasons. The unsaved man simply will not "face up" to the person of Christ and the claims of this One upon his life. And, of course, men even today do not like to be told the truth about themselves, and so they hate Christ for His words. How tragic this is; and yet how typical of the sinful nature of man.

III. Joseph and His Rejection

The story of Joseph's rejection by his brethren is graphically told in Genesis 37. Several points will be noted about the story, all of which are typical of the Lord Jesus Christ.

A. Joseph was sent by his father (37:13). "And Israel said unto Joseph, Do not thy brethren feed the flock in Shechem? come, and I will send thee unto them. And he said to him, Here am I."

In the words quoted above, the mission of Joseph is introduced. His brothers were in far away Shechem with their flocks. The Shechemites were the people who had been involved in the deception of Genesis 34. Jacob, therefore, may have been somewhat concerned that the Shechemites might seek some sort of revenge. So Joseph is sent on this errand of mercy in order to inquire into the well-being of his brethren.

Two things in particular may be noted here which picture Joseph as a type of Christ. First, it should be observed that Joseph was sent by his father with a definite objective in mind. He was to seek out his brothers to inquire after their well-being. He was not to censure them or scold them for their hateful attitude. Instead, he was to inquire after their welfare. Jacob said, "Go, I pray thee, see whether it be well with thy brethren" (37:14). All of this, of course, is typical of Christ, the beloved Son of the Father. He, too, was sent by the Father on an errand of mercy to inquire into our spiritual well-being. He was sent not to censure us or condemn us, but to provide for our salvation. We read in John 3:17, "For God sent not his Son into the world to condemn the world; but that the world through him might be saved."

Second, the prompt and willing obedience of Joseph should also be noted. Upon learning of his father's wishes, Joseph, without hesitation, immediately placed himself at his father's disposal by saying, "Here am I." It is rather significant that no words of protest or reluctance are recorded here of Joseph. He obviously must have known about the hatred and envy of his brethren, and possibly was aware that no good would come of this kind of an errand. Yet willingly and without fear he stood ready to fulfill his father's will. This, too, is typical of Christ. When the time came for the Son of God to take His place in the midst of a world that would hate Him and would be hostile to His coming, He did not hesitate. Instead, like Joseph, He promptly responded, "Here am I." Hebrews 10:7 expresses this willingness: "Then said I, *Lo, I come* (in the volume of the book it is written of me,) *to do thy will, O God.*"

B. Joseph was conspired against (37:18). "And when they saw him afar off, even before he came near unto them, they conspired against him to slay him."

As Joseph approached, the brothers saw an opportunity to vent their spleen on this their annoying "kid brother." They were far from home. No one would ever find out what they had done. So, as he approached, even while he was a great distance away, they conspired against him to kill him.

This, too, is typical of Christ. He, too, was conspired against by His brethren. In Matthew 2, we read that no sooner was Christ born into the world than Herod "conspired" against Him and sought to slay Him. Something of the same took place over and over again during the earthly ministry of Christ. He was conspired against again and again as wicked men sought opportunity to slay Him. Such passages as Matthew 12:14; and 26:3-4 may be used as illustrations.

C. Joseph was sold for money (37:25-28). "Then there passed by Midianites merchantmen; and they drew and lifted Joseph out of the pit, and sold Joseph to the Ishmeelites for twenty pieces of silver" (Gen. 37:28).

The above words record the way in which Joseph was sold by his unfeeling brothers into a life of slavery for 20 pieces of silver. This price was later fixed by Moses as the price of a boy slave (see Lev. 27:5). The parallel, of course, is obvious. Christ was sold into the hands of the Gentiles for 30 pieces of silver. In this connection, it is rather interesting to observe that of the 12 sons of Jacob, it was *Judah* who suggested that Joseph be sold, instead of being left in the pit to die. This becomes rather significant when one stops to realize that it was *Judas* (an anglicized Greek form of the name "Judah"), one of the 12 disciples, who made the horrible bargain to sell the Lord! What a striking parallel this is!

IV. Joseph and His Humiliation

The story of Joseph's humiliation in Egypt is recorded in Genesis 39 and 40. Time does not permit us to point out all of the striking resemblances between this period of Joseph's life and that of the life and ministry of Christ. However, several of the more striking ones will be noted.

A. Joseph became a servant (39:1-2). "And Joseph was brought down to Egypt; and Potiphar, an officer of Pharaoh, captain of the guard, an Egyptian, bought him of the hands of the Ishmeelites . . . and he [Joseph] was in the house of his master the Egyptian."

These words tell how the itinerant traders sold Joseph to Potiphar, the captain of Pharaoh's guard, and a life of slavery was begun. What a contrast this must have been for Joseph!

For years he had been the beloved son of his father's household. And now he was humiliated by being sold as a slave!

The experience of Joseph is but another reminder of the voluntary self-humiliation of the Lord Jesus. Paul spoke of this self-humiliation in Philippians 2:6-7, when he wrote, "Who, being in the form of God, thought it not robbery to be equal with God: but made himself of no reputation, and took upon him the form of a servant." The humiliation of Joseph in Egypt may have been a difficult thing to accept. But it was as nothing in comparison to this voluntary self-humiliation of our Lord.

B. Joseph was sorely tempted (39:7-12). In these verses, the story is told of the immoral advances of Potiphar's wife and Joseph's resolute determination to keep himself pure. What a difficult time of testing this must have been for Joseph. In this connection, it should be noted that Joseph's temptation here is divided into three distinct parts, with each temptation being a bit more severe than the previous one (vv. 7, 10, 12). Yet in spite of the fact that Joseph was sorely tried, he did not sin. Instead, he repulsed every attack of the enemy.

Joseph's experience in temptation again foreshadows the temptation of the Lord Jesus Christ. The writer to the Hebrews spoke of this aspect of our Lord's ministry in Hebrews 4:15 when he wrote of Christ, ". . . but [He] was in all points tempted like as we are, yet without sin." Such passages as Matthew 4:1-11 and Luke 4:1-13 may also be cited as illustrations of this truth.

C. Joseph suffered for the sins of another (39:20–40:23). "And it came to pass, when his [Joseph's] master heard the words of his wife, which she spoke unto him, saying, After this manner did thy servant to me, that his wrath was kindled. And Joseph's master took him, and put him into the prison" (Gen. 39:19-20).

In the above words, Joseph now becomes like Christ in the most important point of all. Though innocent himself, he suffered for the sins of another. Perhaps in this connection the analogy is not quite exact, for the suffering and death of Christ are unique events and cannot be perfectly illustrated or typified. But the idea certainly is here. Just as Joseph suffered innocently for the sins of another, so Christ suffered "the just for the unjust." Many passages may be used to illustrate this important point. The teacher may select any or all of the following: II Corinthians 5:21; I Peter 2:21-22; 3:18.

V. Joseph and His Exaltation

The account of Joseph's exaltation in Egypt along with all of its attendant blessings is recorded in Genesis 41 to 50. Time and space will not permit us to point out all of the parallels between Joseph's exaltation and the exaltation of Christ from this section of Joseph's life. Two or three of the more striking ones, however, are noted here.

A. Joseph was duly exalted (41:39-44). "And Pharaoh said unto Joseph, Forasmuch as God hath shewed thee all this ... thou shalt be over my house, and according unto thy word shall all my people be ruled. ... And Pharaoh said unto Joseph, See, I have set thee over all the land of Egypt" (Gen. 41:39-41).

What a blessed change this must have been for Joseph! Prior to this, he had been abused and mistreated and had suffered innocently for the sins of another. But now he was lifted from the place of shame and humiliation, and was exalted over all the land. Once again, how beautifully this speaks of the One whom Joseph foreshadows. Christ, too, knew by experience the place of shame and humiliation. But He is no longer there. Instead, God has highly exalted Him. Paul speaks of this exaltation in Philippians 2:9-11 where we read, "Wherefore God also hath highly exalted him, and given him a name which is above every name: that at the name of Jesus every knee should bow ... and that every tongue should confess that Jesus Christ is Lord, to the glory of God the Father." See also I Peter 3:22 as a further illustration of the exaltation of Christ.

B. Joseph took a Gentile bride (41:45). "And Pharaoh called Joseph's name Zaphnath-paaneah; and he gave to him to wife Asenath, the daughter of Poti-pherah priest of On."

In these words, we are informed that Joseph, who had been rejected by his brethren, is now further exalted by being given a Gentile bride. Even this, we believe, has its parallel in the life and ministry of Christ. Just as Joseph was rejected by his brethren and now in turn is given a Gentile bride, so Christ was rejected by His brethren according to the flesh, the Jew, and now is in the process of calling out from among the nations of earth, a bride for Himself—the Church, made up largely of Gentiles. See such passages as Acts 15:14 and Ephesians 31 and 32 for the parallel.

C. Joseph was reconciled to his brethren. The heart-moving story of Joseph's reconciliation with his brethren is recorded in Genesis 45. In this chapter, he revealed himself to them and was reconciled to them. And in the chapters that follow, Joseph then became the special guardian and succorer of his brethren in the land.

This incident, too, has its parallel in the life and ministry of Christ. Christ's brethren according to the flesh, the Jews, rejected Him at His first coming. But one day at the end of the age, He will reveal Himself to them as their long-awaited Messiah, and at that time they will be reconciled to Him. The prophet Zechariah spoke of that day in Zechariah 12:10 when he said, "I will pour upon the house of David, and upon the inhabitants of Jerusalem, the spirit of grace and supplications: and they shall look upon me whom they have pierced, and they shall mourn for him, as one mourneth for his only son, and shall be in bitterness for him, as one that is in bitterness for his firstborn." Any number of other passages may be cited as illustrations of the same truth. From that day onward Christ shall become, as was Joseph, the special guardian and succorer of His brethren forever.

CONCLUSION

Our consideration of the story of Joseph brings to a conclusion our studies in the Book of Genesis. And this lesson, with its emphasis on the person of Christ prefigured by Joseph, seems like a fitting theme on which to close. We began our studies in this book by saying that the Book of Genesis is "the seed plot of the Bible." And so it is. Many of the important truths of Scripture which are later developed in greater detail in the Word have their beginnings in this book. In this book, for example, can be found the beginning of man's experience in sin along with all of its various manifestations: ambition, pride, hatred, murder, boasting, polygamy, corruption, violence, drunkenness, indecency, and rebellion against God. And what a sad record all this is. However, in the Book of Genesis can also be found the beginning of God's grace extended toward undeserving, sinful man. In fact, someone has well said that we ought to see more in the Book of Genesis than just a record of human history with all of its disappointing stories of human sin and corruption. Instead, we ought to see in the entire book the gracious hand of God searching, working, and moving in an attempt to lead lost, sinful man back to Himself. This gracious work of God is still not complete. Instead, God, in the person of His Son, is still seeking, working, and moving in an attempt to bring lost men and women to Himself (see Luke 19:10; 15:1-7). God desires, of course, that we should share in this blessed ministry of seeking out those who need Him. And as we place ourselves at His disposal, He is able to do this blessed work. May we so yield ourselves to His control that this blessed ministry which He came to do may be completed.

13

~~~~~~

The Book of Books

INTRODUCTION

    I.   The Old Testament
        A.   The first seventeen books.
        B.   The middle five books.
        C.   The remaining seventeen books.

    II.   The New Testament
        A.   Historical books.
        B.   Church epistles.
        C.   Pastoral epistles.
        D.   General epistles.

CONCLUSION

INTRODUCTION

Many of the great scholars of the world have stated without apology that no man's education is really complete without a working knowledge of the Bible, the Book of Books. And with this statement, we heartily agree. Not only are the contents of the Bible of priceless value, but it's very literary design and beauty are worthy of any man's admiration and attention as well. However, if we are to know the Bible, the Book of Books, then it goes without saying that we must be willing to read and study it faithfully. And this requires work. No man can master any subject without diligent effort, concentration, and application—and this holds good for the Bible. If we are to know its contents and obey its truths, then we must study it faithfully. Much of the criticism of the Bible, we observe, comes from those who have never studied it, or even read it, from beginning to end.

A certain Bible teacher boarded a train and found a seat next to a man who was busily reading his newspaper. Opening his attaché case, the preacher took out his Bible and began to read. The gentleman with the newspaper, glancing out of the corner of his eye, noticed this unusual sight—a passenger reading his Bible on the train! His curiosity got the best of him. And, finally, he leaned over and said, "Pardon me, sir, but are you a minister?" (Funny how folks think that only preachers read their Bibles!) "Yes," said the man, "as a matter of fact, I am a minister." And at that point, he began talking to the man about the Bible, explaining some of its deep mysteries and its marvelous doctrines. After listening intently for some time, the man exclaimed in utter amazement, "How in the world did you ever learn so much about the Bible?" And with tongue in cheek, the Bible teacher simply replied, "Well, I certainly did not get it from reading the daily newspaper!" And do not misunderstand. Certainly we need to be informed. We need to be aware of what is going on in the world around us. But it ought to be a matter of deep concern to us that we spend so much time reading newspapers, magazines, periodicals, and so forth, and so little time in comparison reading the Bible, the Book of Books.

By the way, how much time do you spend reading the Bible? How much time do you spend exploring the pages of this precious book? The answer that you give to this pertinent question will pretty much determine not only your knowledge of the book but your commitment to the Person of the book, Jesus Christ, as well.

Having established the value and the need for exploring the Scriptures, in this concluding study in this series we will present an overview of the Scriptures. It is our observation that many beginning Bible students (more advanced ones, too, for that matter) cannot "see the forest for the trees." They do not see how one part of the Bible fits other parts, and how the various parts make up the whole. To help meet this need, in this, our concluding study of Genesis, the "Book of Beginnings," we will present a "bird's eye view" of the Bible as a whole.

In general terms, our Bible consists of a library of 66 books. These are divided into two major divisions: the Old Covenant Scriptures and the New Covenant Scriptures; or, as we normally call them, the Old and New Testaments. Each of the two testaments, however, is arranged into certain clearly defined, homogenous groups—the Old Testament consisting of 39 books and the New Testament consisting of 27. It will be our purpose in this study to present a broad survey of the flow of Scripture. Specifically, we will want to see how the various parts of the book fit together, how the parts go together to make up the whole, and in the process we will want to emphasize the marvelous evidences of divine order and design running through this, the Book of Books.

I. The Old Testament

A. The first seventeen books. Let's take the Old Testament first. We start with Genesis, Exodus, Leviticus, Numbers, and Deuteronomy. These five books, obviously, comprise a fivefold unit which marks them off as a separate entity. All five books are from the pen of Moses (see Luke 24:44; John 5:45-47). For this reason, they are often referred to as the "Five Books of Moses" or the Pentateuch. The five books are historical in content, and basically they describe the period of the patriarchs and great leaders from Adam to Moses. As to their number, therefore, there are five of them. And as to their nature, they are historical in content.

Next, we look at Joshua, Judges, Ruth, I Samuel, II Samuel, I Kings, II Kings, I Chronicles, II Chronicles, Ezra, Nehemiah, and Esther. Almost instinctively we stop with the Book of Esther without going on to the Book of Job. And we do so because it is apparent to even the casual reader that Job belongs in a very different category. The books of Joshua to Esther, therefore, are 12. They, too, are historical in content, and they basically describe the period of the kings and foreign rulers.

This first stretch of the Old Testament, as we have seen, consists of seventeen historical books, falling into two natural subdivisions of five and twelve. It might be well to observe that there is a further subdivision of the twelve that can be made. The first nine (Joshua to II Chronicles) are a record of Israel's *possession* of the land of Canaan. The last three (Ezra, Nehemiah, and Esther) are the record of Israel's *expulsion* from the land of Canaan and the subsequent return of a remnant. These first seventeen books of the Old Testament might, therefore, be subdivided into five (pre-Canaan), nine (in Canaan), and three (post-exile).

B. The middle five books. Next, we look at Job, Psalms, Proverbs, Ecclesiastes, and Song of Solomon. Once again, no one needs to tell us to make a natural break after the Book of Song of Solomon because the next book in sequence is the prophecy of Isaiah. And the Prophet Isaiah introduces us to a totally different kind of writings, namely, those of the prophets. So Job, Psalms, Proverbs, Ecclesiastes, and Song of Solomon are a fivefold unit that makes up a third major division of the Old Testament. All of the preceding seventeen, as we have noted, are historical in content. But these five are personal and experiential in content. All of the foregoing seventeen are national—they have to do with the beginnings and history of Israel as a nation. These five, however, deal mainly with the personal and individual problems of the human heart. All of the foregoing seventeen were written in prose style. These five, however, are written in poetry. As to their number, therefore, there are five of them. And as to their nature, they are personal and experiential in content.

C. The remaining seventeen books. Finally, we come to another list of 17. This time it is a list of prophetic books: Isaiah, Jeremiah, Lamentations, Ezekiel, Daniel, Hosea, Joel, Amos, Obadiah, Jonah, Micah, Nahum, Habakkuk, Zephaniah, Haggai, Zechariah, Malachi. It is obvious from the contents that these 17 books, too, belong in a category by themselves just as certainly as do the 17 historical books. They form a unit—that of the writings of the prophets.

It is interesting to note, however, that just as the seventeen historical books subdivided into five (the Five Books of Moses) and twelve (Joshua to Esther), so these seventeen prophetic books subdivide into two major divisions. The first five (Isaiah to Daniel) are rightly called the "Major Prophets." And the remaining twelve (Hosea to Malachi) can rightly be classed together and termed the "Minor Prophets." In fact, for centuries the "Minor Prophets" were classed together as one book in the Jewish canon of Scripture and were simply referred to as, "The Twelve" (see Acts 7:42 as an illustration).

It might be argued by some that the division of the writings of the prophets into "Major Prophets" and "Minor Prophets" is an artificial and unwarranted one. This, however, is not the case at all. A careful study of Isaiah, Jeremiah, Ezekiel, and Daniel will show that these books provide the main shape and form of messianic prophecy. Isaiah the prophet, for example, presents the coming of Messiah as both a Suffering Saviour and a Victorious King who will one day rule the world with judgment and with justice. In Jeremiah, we have God's full case against Israel presented, and the Messiah is pictured in this book as a Righteous Branch and as the ultimate Restorer of His people. Ezekiel the prophet looks beyond the immediate judgments upon Israel and sees the Messiah as the perfect Shepherd King under whose glorious rule a perfect temple will one day be erected. And, finally, Daniel presents Messiah as "cut off" without a throne or a kingdom, yet one day standing up upon the smoldering ruins of destroyed Gentile kingdoms and ruling as a universal king. Thus, we are provided with the main shape and form of messianic prophecy. In saying this, it certainly must be recognized that many of the 12 "Minor Prophets" enlarge and amplify on these themes.

A question might be raised regarding the Book of Lamentations. Why does this book, a lament by Jeremiah over the destruction of the Southern Kingdom, appear in the writings of the prophets? To many, Lamentations is little more than a poetic postscript to the writings of Jeremiah. But not so. To the contrary, the Book of Lamentations belongs in a category all by itself. It memorializes one of the most important events in human history—the destruction of Jerusalem and the scattering of God's chosen people, a scattering from which they have never been fully regathered, even after 2,500 years. In addition, it is interesting to note that Lamentations occupies a unique place in the arrangement of the Old Testament Scriptures. Lamentations is the "center point" of the Major Prophets. It divides Isaiah and Jeremiah from Ezekiel and Daniel. And that is significant. Isaiah and Jeremiah were two of the great pre-exile prophets, while Ezekiel and Daniel were two of the great post-exile prophets. Lamentations, therefore, is the dividing point between these two great periods of history. And it does so by memorializing the destruction of Jerusalem and the scattering of God's chosen people.

One further comment about the Minor Prophets before we leave them: as we have seen, the last twelve of the seventeen historical books further subdivide themselves into nine and three. The first nine (Joshua–II Chronicles) are pre-exilic, and the remaining three (Ezra, Nehemiah, and Esther) are post-exilic. And so it is with these twelve Minor Prophets. The first nine (Hosea-Zephaniah) are pre-exilic, and the remaining three (Haggai, Zechariah, and Malachi) are post-exilic.

The thirty-nine books of the Old Testament, therefore, fall into an orderly grouping. First, there are seventeen historical books. Next, there are five personal and experiential books. And, finally, the Old Testament canon closes with seventeen prophetic books. And as we have observed, both "seventeens" can be subdivided into "fives" and "nines" and "threes." Is all of this mere accident? Or, is it evidence of order and design? Think about it for a moment. Even more amazing is the fact that the Old Testament was written by over 30 writers spaced out over a period of 1,200 years. They wrote in different places, to different persons, for different purposes. Not one of them ever dreamed that his writings would be preserved for all generations to read and appreciate—to say nothing of becoming a part of that amazing unity that we call the Old Testament. Yet, it happened. And as we reflect on that, we cannot help but believe that behind those earthly, human writers there is divine order and design. God planned this book. He gave it to us by His grace as a final, complete, and authoritative revelation of Himself. And it is ours to study, to obey, and to make a part of our lives.

II. The New Testament

We turn our attention now to the New Testament. And in much the same way, we find clear, unmistakable evidences of divine order and design.

A. Historical books. First, we take a brief look at Matthew, Mark, Luke, John, and Acts. These five are the only historical books of the New Testament. And as such, they are foundational to everything else that follows. Therefore, they stand together as a clearly defined unit.

The question often arises, "Why are there four Gospels? Would not one straightforward, continuous narrative have been better? Would this not have made things clearer and more precise? In addition, might not such a narrative have saved us from many of the difficulties that have arisen over what some have said are 'conflicting accounts'?" The answer to the question is quite plain. No one, or even two, accounts of the life of Christ would have given us a complete portrayal of His Person and work. You see, there are four distinct offices of Christ portrayed in the four Gospels. He is presented as King in Matthew, Servant in Mark, Son of Man in Luke, and Son of God in John. Certainly it is true that each of the four Gospels has much in common with the others. Each deals with the earthly life of Christ: His teachings, His miracles, His death, His resurrection, and so on. But each Gospel has its differences, too. And no one writer presents a complete picture. So, the four become a practical necessity.

To illustrate, in the National Gallery in London, England, on a single canvas there are three paintings of King Charles I. In one, his head is turned to the left; in another, to the right; and in the center is a full-face view. The story behind the painting is that the famous painter Van Dyck painted them for Bernini, the Roman sculptor, that he might, with their help, be able to produce a bust of the king. By combining impressions of all three paintings, Bernini was able to produce a suitable likeness. One view was not enough. And just so, the Gospels are intended to serve the same purpose. Each presents a different aspect of Christ's ministry. And together we have in them a complete picture of His glorious Person. He was a King, but at the same time a Perfect Servant. He was the Son of Man. But we must never forget that He was also the Son of God.

In this first stretch of the New Testament, therefore, there are five historical books. Four of them present a different aspect of Christ's ministry. And one (Acts) presents His continuing ministry through the lives of His committed followers.

B. Church epistles. Next comes a group of letters that plainly adhere together as a common entity. It is a group of epistles that are all addressed to Christian churches. They are: Romans, I Corinthians, II Corinthians, Galatians, Ephesians, Philippians, Colossians, I Thessalonians, and II Thessalonians. All were written by Paul, the apostle. His letters to the churches at Thessalonica, Galatia, Corinth, and Rome were written while on his various missionary journeys. Ephesians, Philippians, and Colossians were written while Paul was a prisoner in Rome.

Once again, in these several books we need to see the Christo-centric character of the Bible. All of the Bible, essentially, is about Him. His face and His glorious Person ought to be seen on every page. And so it is with these books. In all of these epistles, Christ is the central Person, and each book presents a different aspect of His Person and work:

Romans—Jesus Christ, our Righteousness
I Corinthians—Jesus Christ, our Lord
II Corinthians—Jesus Christ, our Sufficiency
Galatians—Jesus Christ, our Liberty
Ephesians—Jesus Christ, our All-In-All
Philippians—Jesus Christ, our Joy
Colossians—Jesus Christ, our Life
I Thessalonians—Jesus Christ, our Coming One
II Thessalonians—Jesus Christ, our Returning Lord

Here, then, is the second great span of New Testament books—the church epistles. And, once again, note their number and their nature. As to their number, there are nine of them. And as to their nature, they are primarily doctrinal in content.

C. Pastoral epistles. Next, we come to four short letters that form another little grouping: I Timothy, II Timothy, Titus, Philemon. These four brief letters are not addressed to

Christian churches, as such. Rather, they are addressed to individuals. And their purpose is primarily pastoral. They were written to guide men in the pastoral care of churches.

Once more, it is refreshing to see the Person and work of Christ as central in this section of Scripture. Jesus Christ, our Teacher is presented in I Timothy; and II Timothy portrays Jesus Christ, our Example. In Titus, He is depicted as our Pattern. And, finally, in Philemon, Jesus Christ is presented to us as our Lord and Master. How important that we see Him on every page!

D. General epistles. Finally, we have one more grouping of nine books. They are: Hebrews, James, I Peter, II Peter, I John, II John, III John, Jude, and Revelation. These nine are not addressed to specific Christian churches in quite the same sense as are the other nine. Rather, some are addressed to Hebrew Christians (Hebrews, James, and I Peter); others are addressed to the church at large (II Peter, I John, and Jude); two are addressed to individuals (II and III John); and the final letter (Revelation) is really a letter from Christ Himself! (see Revelation 1:1). For these reasons, we group these final nine books into one category and call them "General Epistles."

Following through on our earlier observation that the entire Bible is Christo-centric, in these books, too, we see the Person and work of Christ clearly:

> Hebrews—Jesus Christ, our Intercessor
> James—Jesus Christ, our Pattern
> I Peter—Jesus Christ, Chief Cornerstone of our Faith
> II Peter—Jesus Christ, our Strength
> I John—Jesus Christ, our Life
> II John—Jesus Christ, the Truth
> III John—Jesus Christ, the Way
> Jude—Jesus Christ, our Keeper
> Revelation—Jesus Christ, Our Triumphant King

In all of this, again, we see evidences of divine order and design. On this point, someone has very wisely likened the New Testament to a beautiful archway. The five historical books (Matthew—Acts) provide a solid foundation upon which to build. On either side of the foundation are two groups of "nines" rising up like beautifully sculptured pillars (the nine church epistles and the nine general epistles). These two pillars are securely connected together and arched by four pastoral epistles (I Timothy—Philemon). And all of them together lead us to the precious Person and work of Jesus Christ. Did all of this happen by accident? Or, is it evidence of design? Think about it. The New Testament, too, was written by a succession of writers (at least eight of them) who wrote from different places, to different persons, and for different purposes. Yet, the parts fit together beautifully and completely so as to present one complete message. They are a complete, final, and authoritative revelation of the unique Person and work of Jesus Christ. The inevitable conclusion is that "someone" planned this book. That "Someone" was none other than God Himself. And He has given us the Book that we might read it, study it, and make it a part of our lives.

CONCLUSION

If the Bible is the very Word of God (and it is), then the applications are rather obvious.

For those of us who are Christians, this means that we need to be loyal to the Word of God as never before. We must preach it from our pulpits. We must expound it in our seminaries. We must print it in our publishing houses. We must declare it on the mission fields of the world. We must speak of it on our streets and in the neighborhoods of our cities. We must read it in our homes. We must teach it to our children. We must study it thoughtfully and prayerfully in the privacy of our own rooms. And then we must obey it and submit to its authority and live by its teachings. And this we must do until Jesus calls us home.

For those unsaved, a similar application can be made.

Those outside of Christ need to give the Word of God a chance in their lives. You see, if the Bible is the very Word of God (and it is), then its message is true. What it says about sin is true. What it says about God's love is true. What it says about coming judgment is true. And what it says about the work of Christ and the invitation of the Gospel is also true. If so, the most sensible and reasonable decision that a man could make on the basis of these facts would be for him to repent of his sin, give his heart to Christ, and then to obey the Word of God for the rest of his days. That's what men need to do with the Book of Books. May it be so as men love and share this precious message.

ADDITIONAL STUDY GUIDES IN THIS SERIES ...

DEUTERONOMY, Bernard N. Schneider, paper, $2.95.

JOSHUA, JUDGES & RUTH, John J. Davis, paper, $2.95.

I & II SAMUEL & I KINGS 1-11, John J. Davis, cloth, $4.95; paper, $3.95.

KINGS & CHRONICLES, John C. Whitcomb, cloth, $3.95; paper, $2.95.

PROVERBS, Charles W. Turner, paper, $2.95.

GOSPEL OF JOHN, Homer A. Kent, Jr., cloth, $4.95; paper, $3.95.

ACTS, Homer A. Kent, Jr., paper, $3.95.

ROMANS, Herman A. Hoyt, paper, $2.95.

I CORINTHIANS, James L. Boyer, cloth, $3.95; paper, $2.95.

GALATIANS, Homer A. Kent, Jr., paper, $2.95.

EPHESIANS, Tom Julien, paper, $2.95.

PHILIPPIANS, David L. Hocking, paper, $2.95.

I & II TIMOTHY, Dean Fetterhoff, paper, $2.95.

HEBREWS, Herman A. Hoyt, paper, $2.50.

JAMES, Roy R. Roberts, paper, $3.50.

I, II, III, JOHN, Raymond E. Gingrich, paper, $2.95.

REVELATION, Herman A. Hoyt, paper, $2.95.

THE WORLD OF UNSEEN SPIRITS, Bernard N. Schneider, paper, $2.95.

THE HOLY SPIRIT AND YOU, Bernard N. Schneider, paper, $3.95.

PROPHECY, THINGS TO COME, James L. Boyer, paper, $2.95.

PULPIT WORDS TRANSLATED FOR PEW PEOPLE, Charles W. Turner, paper, $2.95.

Order from your local Christian bookstore or BMH Books, P. O. Box 544, Winona Lake, IN 46590. (Include a check with your order and BMH Books pays all postage charges.)